About the author

Dr John F Ashton holds research degrees in the areas of Science and Philosophy. He was awarded the Institute of Educational Research Prize at the University of Newcastle for his PhD thesis which outlined a holographic model for the interpretation of scientific data.

Dr Ashton has applied the holographic principle to the well-documented evidence of dreams and premonitions which have revealed the future. His research has led him to the fascinating conclusion that a cosmic intelligence oversees the events in our lives and the destiny of our planet.

Dr Ashton is a Fellow of the Royal Australian Chemical Institute and is the author of several highly successful books in the area of environment and health.

THE
SEVENTH
MILLENNIUM

THE EVIDENCE THAT WE CAN KNOW THE FUTURE

Dr John F Ashton

NEW
HOLLAND

To my wonderful children Alice, Nathan, Andrew and Kathryn.

First published in Australia in 1998 by
New Holland Publishers Pty Ltd
Sydney • Auckland • London • Cape Town

14 Aquatic Drive Frenchs Forest NSW 2086 Australia
1A, 218 Lake Road Northcote Auckland New Zealand
24 Nutford Place London W1H 6DQ United Kingdom
80 McKenzie Street Cape Town 8001 South Africa

Project Co-ordinator: Anna Sanders
Editor: Glenda Downing
Designer: Laurence Lemmon-Warde
Typesetter: Midland Typesetters
Printer: McPhersons Printing Group

National Library of Australia Cataloguing-in-Publication Data:

Ashton, John F
The seventh millennium: the evidence that we can know the future.

Bibilography
Includes index.
ISBN 1 86436 359 2.

1. Forecasting. I. Title.

133.3

Cover image © Terry Musgrove

Contents

Acknowledgments

I wish to express my sincere thanks to Mrs Alison Buckley BA, DipEd for her valuable criticism and comments; my wife, Colleen, who cheerfully and with great care typed the manuscript.

John F Ashton

Foreword

Modern science got into its stride around AD1500. Early devotees of this 'new' science included Copernicus, Galileo, Leibnitz, Descartes and the grand master, Isaac Newton. It was a remarkable movement and transformed our earthly society. However, while many aspects of the transformation were good, others were not so good.

By the 1950s most aspects of life in advanced societies had been affected by these changes. Penicillin, for example, was being hailed as a 'wonder drug'. Nuclear fission, on the other hand, had been discovered and nuclear weapons were in the hands of regimes that were far from perfect. Also, the world's population was beginning to outstrip the Earth's natural resources.

A great deal of modern science is based on physics, but physics itself is a divided science. On the one side there is quantum mechanics, and on the other side, the criticism of quantum mechanics by Albert Einstein, and his colleagues Podolsky and Rosen. In addition, there is the work of two modern, intellectual giants—Wolfgang Pauli and Carl Gustav Jung. Their remarkable work *The Interpretation of Nature and the Psyche* takes into account the possibility that there are levels of consciousness higher than the material level that allow for the explanation of phenomena beyond the reach of physics.

To explain these phenomena, such as the incidences described in this book (and incidentally save our planet), we need a higher level of science. One such possibility is outlined in *The Seventh Millennium*. I strongly recommend that you read it.

Emeritus Professor Brian McCusker D.Sc. M.R.I.A
Formerly Professor of High Energy Nuclear Physics, University of Sydney

Preface

For thousands of years humans have wondered about the future, often looking for portents in the moon and stars or in the other signs in nature. Some people have actually seen the future, in dreams or visions.

Glimpses of the future have been as detailed and accurate for some as to suggest that the future already exists, perhaps in a dimension of space not limited by time as we know it.

Scientific studies have recently confirmed that some people have the ability to see the future with varying degrees of accuracy. This opens a whole new area of human knowledge that affects our lives. If we can know the future can we still change it if we don't like certain aspects? If the future exists, do we really have freedom of choice? Are we unknowingly driven by destiny fields like migrating birds and butterflies that have never known their parents or their destination?

As a new millennium unfolds, many people have doubts and fears about our future—the increasing levels of environmental pollution, the destruction of the ozone layer, the greenhouse effect, the threat of nuclear war and radioactive fallout, the possibility of the spread of deadly viruses and the continued increase in the human population all point to a gloomy future.

But is this the actual future mapped out for our planet? Can the prophecies for the next millennium provide the clues for pathways to our achieving the best future for ourselves and our children?

This book puts together a fascinating puzzle which suggests that our choices now can affect the future but only within preordained limits.

Introduction

'What does the future hold?' This question embraces a basic curiosity common to all of us. The success of a business venture, the endurance of a relationship, and deciding from an array of career choices: these are some of the many common matters where definite guidance would be helpful.

Of course, information of one form or another is readily available in most modern Western cultures. For example, many newspapers and popular magazines have their 'Today's Stars' or 'This Month's Horoscope' page where readers can look up their star signs and read the forecast of the day, week or month. Some radio stations have their own psychics, and listeners can phone in and have their lives analysed and their questions about the future of their relationships, families and finances answered. In a large city such as Sydney, fortune-tellers practice openly and a wide clientele consult palm readers, astrologers, numerologists and tarot practitioners.

But can clairvoyants really see the future in a crystal ball? Is it actually possible for us to know the future? As a practising research scientist I did not take claims of fortune-telling seriously, but during Easter 1994, while gold prospecting with friends at Sofala in New South Wales, I was told an outstanding example of a person seeing the future in vivid detail. This story stimulated my research into the fascinating puzzle of the future.

I was sitting at the campfire with two business friends and our families sharing stories. Mike, who owned a kitchen manufacturing business, told us of an unusually vivid dream he had in 1986 which had helped save the life of his wife several weeks later.

Mike had moved his family and business to the Atherton Tablelands in northern Queensland. The area is rich dairy country with beautiful, undulating green hills. Like most people Mike often had vivid dreams but one night his dream was unusually so. The setting could have been anywhere in the Tablelands. He saw a car leave the road at a bend and go up an embankment. It came to rest on its roof at the edge of a steep drop on the other side of the ridge. When Mike woke up the next morning he could not remember how the car went up the bank but he could recall very clearly the position of the car and the details of the scenery at the setting of the accident. In the dream he had sensed a very strong smell of molasses grass and, strangely, although the accident occurred at night he saw it as a daytime scene. He also recalled feeling that this was no ordinary dream, that somehow it had significance and was 'personal'. Although the dream bothered him, Mike decided not to tell his wife, Marie, about it.

Several weeks later, a close friend by the name of Owen was to fly down to Sydney for tests for a bone marrow transplant. The evening before he was to fly out Marie decided to drive over to see Owen's family to deliver some books she had promised. At about 9 pm Owen phoned Mike to see if Marie was still coming with the books as he needed to get to bed. Mike immediately knew that something serious had happened to Marie. She had left three and a half hours earlier at about 5.30 pm and the drive was only about an hour. He recalled his vivid dream and described the accident scene to Owen, including the smell of the molasses grass. Straightaway Owen said he knew the exact location, which was only about 15 minutes from his home. He arranged to meet Mike there. When Mike arrived at the scene, Marie's car was on its roof up a six-metre embankment on the edge of a steep drop and out of sight from the road—exactly as he had seen it in his dream. In the air was the characteristic smell of nearby molasses grass, which on this particular part of the road was noticeably strong. The car had obviously turned head over tail as well as rolled and was extensively damaged. Owen had arrived before him to find Marie walking dazed along the road just below the crashed car. She had regained consciousness only a few minutes before, and had crawled down the bank to the road. He took her straight away to the Millaa Millaa medical centre, where she was transferred to an ambulance and taken to Atherton Hospital. On this journey she lost consciousness again.

At the hospital the doctors told Mike it was a miracle she was alive. Marie's neck should have been broken as during the accident her head was forced onto her chest with such impact that the impression of her face could still be seen. Later, after leaving hospital, Marie could not recall how the accident occurred, and the cause of it was never determined.

When I heard this story, I was impressed by this particularly powerful example of precognition. Mike had seen the future in vivid detail—complete with smells—weeks ahead of the actual occurrence. The incident had been a major event in his life. The dream had enabled Marie's whereabouts to be located exactly on an unlit country road, and in time to prevent possible further serious injury occurring. The other interesting feature of his experience was that Mike had sensed beforehand that the dream was different from regular dreams, that it had special significance.

As I thought about Mike's experience it seemed to me that here was very strong evidence that somehow the future existed and under certain conditions could be viewed by the human mind. Some people report having had a number of glimpses of the future in dreams. A computer engineer servicing the terminals at the research laboratories where I work, after hearing about my precognition research, told me that often he would be in a street somewhere and remember seeing the exact setting in a dream weeks or months beforehand. Nothing unusual occurred in these dreams: they were ordinary happenings in his life seen in detail ahead of time.

The sense of having previously experienced something when encountering it for the first time is commonly referred to as *déjà vu*. These experiences are clearly different from the experience of premonitions, which are intense feelings often of warning about a future event. For example, after the Aberfan mine disaster in Wales in 1966, in which coal slag from a mine slid down a hill and covered a school killing 144 children and teachers, 76 reports were collected from people who claimed to have had premonitions of the accident. Twenty-four of these premonitions had been witnessed by another person before the event.[1]

I have also experienced this sort of premonition. In 1973, as a postgraduate research fellow at the University of Tasmania, I was driving home one bleak rainy evening when I experienced a powerful feeling that I needed to slow down. I argued with myself that I was not exceeding the speed limit and decided to slow down only slightly as I approached a green traffic light. I did not want to have to stop if the light changed to red. As I reached the inter-section, I saw a sports car travelling at high speed along the cross road. There was no time for me to stop on the slippery road and the sports car, driven at high speed through the red light, clipped the very front driver's side of my car, spinning the car through 90 degrees. The sports car continued on fish-tailing down the street for some distance. If I had not slowed down just marginally as I did, I probably would have received a direct side-on hit and suffered serious injuries. On the other hand, if I had believed my premonition and slowed down considerably, the other car would have run the red light well ahead of me and I would not have been in danger at all. When I reported the accident at the Hobart police station some minutes later, they were already looking for the sports car as the accident had been reported by a witness.

Another similar incident occurred in December 1979. I was driving along a narrow, winding country road south of Hobart when my four-year-old daughter suddenly became very distraught and called out 'Slow down, Daddy. Please slow down' as we approached a blind corner on the hillside. Again I was well under the speed limit, but for the sake of my daughter I began to slow down. As we entered the bend an oncoming car had cut the corner at speed and was travelling towards us on the wrong side of the road. It crashed past the front mudguard of our car before careering off the road, through a fence and into a paddock. No-one was hurt in the accident, but if I had not slowed down in response to my daughter's pleas we would have been involved in a head-on collision. My daughter had experienced a powerful premonition of imminent danger.

My daughter had never previously been in an accident and had been travelling in cars since she was a baby. This was the first and only time she had ever behaved in this way. She began crying out probably about 30 seconds before we reached the blind corner. We were travelling at about 40 kilometres per hour on a rough gravel road and I estimate that the oncoming car, which was being driven by an underage male driver, was travelling at least 70 kilometres per hour. On the basis of calculation, the other car was about one kilometre away from us when my daughter experienced her premonition. At this stage the youthful driver would not have been in sight of the bend, and it is highly unlikely that he would have been thinking of cutting the corner. Yet, my daughter received a telepathic signal. She did not sense the future as such but rather imminent danger which could be averted. That is, it was a possible future outcome which was almost completely averted by my action of slightly reducing my speed. (The mudguard of our car was damaged but we were able to drive home.)

My experience six years earlier admits of a similar interpretation. At the moment when I first received the impression that I needed to slow down, the traffic light would still have been out of sight to the other driver because of curves in the road he was travelling on. So it is unlikely that I received some sort of telepathic intent to run the red light from the other driver. Instead, both incidents seem to evince an interpretation that there was an external observer 'mind' who saw the overall situation. The revelation showed that in both incidents the cars were on a collision course and the observer communicated directly to the minds of my daughter and myself. Such an observer may be outside time and space as we know it and may fit the description of what is commonly referred to as an 'angel'. I shall look more closely at the accumulating evidence for 'angels' and the role they may play in seeing the future a little later in this chapter.

Sometimes premonitions are separated from the event more by space rather than by time. That is, we experience intense feelings about an event which is currently taking place some distance away. One such example which I read about in the newspaper particularly impressed me. It happened during the English soccer tragedy at Hillsborough soccer stadium on 15 April 1989 in which 95 people were crushed to death and nearly 1000 fans were injured when the crowd stampeded.

As I recall the report, a father had taken his young son to the soccer match while his wife had taken their two young daughters to see a movie. While watching the film the mother was suddenly overcome with feelings of a terrible loss and of life being crushed out. These feelings were so intense and overwhelming that she took her two daughters out of the cinema and caught the bus home, where she immediately turned on the radio. When she heard the news of the tragedy she sensed that her husband and son were among the victims. A short while later the police arrived with the tragic news that her husband and son had been crushed to death. The body of the young boy was found under that of his father who, being a heavily built man of close to two metres in height, had tried in vain to shield his son from the weight of the crowd. The emotional bonding between a husband and wife or mother and child can be particularly strong, and it is revealing that in this instance the premonition signals experienced by the mother were so strong as to swamp the powerful visual and audio signals her mind was receiving while watching a film.

I recall another similar case which was reported on television in Sydney. The mother of a young man who had committed suicide by jumping off a multistorey car park in the city was interviewed on the news. The woman told how she was shopping in the supermarket when she experienced a profound feeling that something horrible had happened to her son. She left the supermarket and went home where, soon after, she was contacted by the police. The time of her son's death corresponded with the time she experienced distress in the supermarket. Again the signals she received were sufficiently strong to interrupt her activities.

Signals received by the mind can be so clear as to constitute a sort of remote viewing. An example of this phenomenon was reported in 1848 and confirmed by a number of independent witnesses.[2] On 9 September, at the siege of Mooltan near the North-West Frontier Province of India, a major-general was severely wounded. Thinking himself to be dying, he requested that his ring be taken off and sent to his wife. She, meanwhile, was in Ferozepore, 240 kilometres away, resting on her bed. She distinctly saw in her mind her husband being carried off the battlefield and clearly heard his voice saying, 'Take this ring off my finger and send it to my wife'.

This case is different from the more common examples of telepathy where the thoughts of one human mind are somehow transferred to another human mind. Instead, the wife saw the scene not as her husband would have viewed the situation but rather as a nearby observer or onlooker close enough to hear the voice of the wounded soldier.

There seems to be evidence that telepathic powers where a message can be sent deliberately from one person to another via the mind only, are prevalent among primitive peoples and that these powers have been lost as civilisation develops. I have heard of a number of reports by educators and social workers of telepathy being commonplace among remote Aboriginal Australian tribes. John Taylor, Professor of Mathematics at King's College in London, reported in his study of telepathy that communities on the island of Bali apparently possessed telepathic powers until very recently.[3]

So far we have discussed examples of people having seen the future as well as the present from some distance away. The next obvious question to ask is can we also see the past? John Taylor describes the amazing accounts of a woman whom it appears had the ability to see the past when under hypnosis.

In one account she described details of the life of a woman who was murdered in York, England, in 1190. The subject claimed that the woman had died in the crypt of a church in York. This church was later identified by an eminent historian as St Mary's, Castlegate, using the subject's description of the location. However, the crypt was not discovered until some months later when a workman found it under the chapel of the church.

In another experience, this same subject saw details of a servant named Alison who served a man called Jacques Coeur in fifteenth-century France. The subject told how:

> At the end of the passage with the portraits and pictures he has a room where he keeps his porcelain and jade and he has a beautiful golden apple with jewels in it. He said it was given to him by the Sultan of Turkey.

The man Jacques Coeur did exist 'as a real person—a wealthy merchant, financier and adviser to Charles VII of France'. No historians could identify the golden apple until one said that he had discovered, in an obscure list of items confiscated from Jacques Coeur by the Treasury, a 'grenade' of gold; *grenade* is the French word for pomegranate—very much like an apple.[4] The fine detail of the accounts suggest that the subject did somehow see the past during these experiences and that either the past exists outside conventional space-time or, alternatively, a mind which is outside conventional space-time communicated the details via a telepathy-type process.

Taylor also mentions a study which documented 1600 cases of people who have had experiences of seeing the past in detail.[5] These types of experiences are often interpreted as memories of a previous life and hence evidence of reincarnation. I shall discuss in more detail in later chapters how these retrocognitive visions of the past share many similarities with precognitive dreams of future events and with telepathic experiences of events taking place some distance away. Collectively, these phenomena appear to provide important clues about the nature of an existence field, outside space and time as we know it, which appears to order the processes that make up our existence, much like a gravitational field directs the paths of falling objects.

If unknown future or distant events can affect our dreams, our feelings and the thoughts of our mind, can our mind in turn affect distant or future events?

In the late 1970s and early 1980s, Robert G Jahn, Professor of Aerospace Sciences and Dean Emeritus of the School of Engineering and Applied Science at Princeton University, together with Brenda J Dunne, the manager of the Princeton Engineering Anomalies Research Laboratory, carried out thousands of experiments to test this hypothesis. In one set of experiments 9000 balls fell through a device which distributed them into a bell-shaped pile around a centre mean point.

A subject was asked to sit in front of the machine and concentrate his thinking to make more balls fall on the right side of the centre mean point. Each subject was asked to repeat the experiment hundreds of times. When the results were analysed statistically, the number of times there was an excess of balls in the direction intended by the subject significantly exceeded the number predicted by chance.

In other words, the balls would fall in a symmetrical bell shape around the centre when the subject had neutral thoughts, but when the subject concentrated his thoughts to make the balls fall to one side they tended to fall in a distorted bell shape more times than one would expect to happen by chance. The researchers reported 'we find a pattern of small but numerous shifts of the mean compounding to an overall accumulation of significant anomaly'.[6]

Jahn and Dunne describe a number of other experiments carried out at Princeton University which provide strong evidence for a weak mind–machine interaction. At first glance these experiments seem to have little bearing on our understanding of the future. They are very significant, however, because they clearly demonstrate effects that cannot be adequately explained by the mechanical space-time model which underpins conventional science. Furthermore, the results suggest that a scientist may actually affect the readings of what was otherwise thought to be an objective instrument of measurement. For example, a scientist who strongly believes a certain rock to be very old may be able to cause the dating instrument to shift to give an inaccurate reading that indicates an older age. Many scientists would be uncomfortable with this thought, however, the Princeton University research cannot be lightly dismissed and will be discussed in more detail later in this book.

The research of Jahn and Dunne found that the mind–machine interactions varied with each subject, with some subjects able to produce much stronger effects than others. At the time of writing their book, of the 22 subjects who had been tested, only eight had generated databases of anomalous effects significant enough to suggest that the human mind was influencing the machine.[7]

Of course the concept that our minds can change events, particularly the future, is not new. Since ancient times people have prayed to God or the gods in the belief that the human mind can make contact with a superior mind who is all-powerful and who can not only see the future as well as the present but can change the future or perform miracles in response to prayer. Down through the ages religious books have presented numerous stories of answers to prayer and there is an abundance of modern accounts.[8] A S Maxwell recounts a number of stories of answers to prayer during the Second World War told by military chaplains. Some of the stories involved high-ranking army and navy personnel.[9]

An outstanding example of detailed records of continuous answers to prayer for over a century involved the running of a world-famous orphanage at Bristol in England. The orphanage was begun by George Muller in 1833 and continued running under the direction of a board long after Muller died in 1898 at the age of 93. Muller depended solely on prayer to provide the needs for running the orphanage and caring for more than 17 000 orphans during that period.[10] He kept an amazing, detailed journal of his prayers and the answers to those prayers until he died, including details of every donation received to run the orphanage. In the early days of the orphanage, when he and his staff were caring for about 2000 children, he often wrote that they had no food for breakfast and no money. He would call his staff to prayer, sometimes for hours, and without fail someone would come with a donation at least sufficient to buy food for the orphans for that day, or food itself would be donated.[11] On occasions the money needed would arrive by mail from places as far away as the East Indies.[12] Muller's tradition of praying for the needs of the orphanage was continued by the trustees of the institution up until the Second World War. The 1938–39 annual report of the institution gave the income for the year as £34 322.8.9. There was also a balance on hand of £712.4.9½. The report concludes:

Without anyone having been personally applied to by us for a donation, £2,369,747.12.8¾ has been received for the Orphans, as a result of prayer to God, since the commencement of the work, which sum includes the amount received for the Building Fund for the five Houses. Besides this, articles of clothing, furniture, etc., and of food have been given in great variety for the use of the Orphans.[13]

It is incredible that a large orphanage could be run for 105 years without a source of income or asking anyone for money. Yet requests made by praying staff on an as-needed basis drew unsolicited donations equivalent in today's terms to more than $50 million.

From a scientific viewpoint, this constitutes a massive amount of consistent evidence of the power of the human mind. There is the temptation to think that the prayers of George Muller and his staff were just like sending out telepathic messages for help which were received by other persons who responded by sending money, food and so forth. If this were the case, however, one could imagine quite a number of people responding at any one time. Clearly, from the financial records and Muller's journal, this was not the case. Instead the responses seem to have been regulated or filtered in such a way that excessive amounts of money or food (such as bread and meat which would not keep long anyway) were not received. In other words, the responses fit the criteria of being managed by an observing mind outside our understanding of time and space. Further evidence for this comes from the cases where specific sums of money were sent from overseas months *in advance* of the prayer request being made. This mail was carried by sailing ship yet arrived just at the right time, often to the very day. The response to the human mind was being prepared months in advance.

I have also heard of a number of cases where prayer has affected machines. One outstanding example was recorded by Dr Francis Schaeffer, the eminent philosopher and lecturer who wrote the environmental classic *Pollution and the Death of Man*.[14] In an earlier work Schaeffer wrote of a personal experience:

Once I was flying at night over the North Atlantic. It was 1947, and I was coming back from my first visit to Europe. Our plane, one of those old DC4s with two engines on each wing, was within two or three minutes of the middle of the Atlantic. Suddenly two engines on one wing stopped. I had already flown a lot, and so I could feel the engines going wrong. I remember thinking, if I'm going to go down into the ocean, I'd better get my coat. When I did, I said to the hostess, 'There's something wrong with the engines.' She was a bit snappy and said, 'You people always think there's something wrong with the engines.' So I shrugged my shoulders, but I took my coat. I had no sooner sat down, than the lights came on and a very agitated co-pilot came out. 'We're in trouble,' he said. 'Hurry and put on your life jackets.'

So down we went, and we fell and fell, until in the middle of the night with no moon we could actually see the water breaking under us in the darkness. And as we were coming down, I prayed. Interestingly enough, a radio message had gone out, an SOS that was picked up and broadcast immediately all over the United States in a flash news announcement: 'There is a plane falling in the middle of the Atlantic.' My wife heard about this and at once she gathered our three little girls together and they knelt down and began to pray. They were praying in St Louis, Missouri, and I was praying on the plane. And we were going down and down. Then, while we could see the waves breaking beneath us and everyone was ready for the crash, suddenly the two motors started, and we went on into Gander. When we got down I found the pilot and asked what happened. 'Well,' he said, 'it's a strange thing, something we can't explain. Only rarely do two motors stop on one wing, but you can make an absolute rule that when they do, they don't start again. We don't understand it.' So I turned to him and I said, 'I can explain it.' He looked at me: 'How?' And I said, 'My Father in heaven started it because I was praying.' That man had the strangest look on his face and he turned away.[15]

Schaeffer's interpretation of this event is that the human mind can communicate with the God (mind) who created the universe and that this mind can interact with the physical world and in this case start the plane engines.[16] This is an example of a situation which, by the admission of the pilot, does not have a mechanical explanation. It is outside the realm of conventional science. The engines in the plane had stopped, then some time later just before the plane was about to crash into the sea the engines started again. In the words of the pilot: 'It's a strange thing, something we can't explain.'

Generally, when events like this occur they are either ignored by science or the scientist commits an act of faith and believes that there must have been some rare mechanical explanation. However, as we have seen from the Princeton University research, the examples where this sort of answer to prayer or mind–matter interaction occurs can provide valuable clues to our understanding of a reality outside of conventional space-time.

Dr Ben Carson, the world famous paediatric brain surgeon at Johns Hopkins University Hospital, also believes that prayer can affect future outcomes in the real world. In 1987, Dr Carson gained worldwide recognition for his part in the first successful separation of Siamese twins joined at the back of the head. This was an extremely complex and delicate operation, one of five months' planning and 22 hours of actual surgery, involving a surgical plan that Carson helped initiate. Carson is well known for taking on brain operations that other professionals see as too difficult or hopeless. However, Carson requests that all patients and their families say their prayers for a successful outcome before surgery. He believes that prayer really works.[17]

Interesting outcomes have also occurred when a whole country has been called to pray in the face of a national emergency. In August 1914, during the First World War, the British people were called to a national day of prayer because the future of the Allied forces looked bleak. Following this a number of remarkable incidents occurred which held back the German forces long enough to allow the British army to withdraw to comparative safety.

One such incident occurred at Mons, in Belgium, during a battle between the German and Allied armies on 23 and 24 August 1914. The British army, greatly outnumbered by German forces, found itself under heavy attack and suffering severe losses. Since there were practically no reserve forces, serious defeat looked inevitable and the *Times* correspondent prematurely telegraphed unnecessarily alarming news that the British army had been 'annihilated at Mons'.[18] However, next day news came that the disaster had been averted by a miraculous turn of events, involving angels.

Captain Cecil W Haywood, Staff Officer in the 1st Corps Intelligence, British Army Headquarters, gave the following report:

While a detachment of British soldiers was retiring through Mons under very heavy gun-fire, they knelt behind a hastily erected barricade and endeavoured to hold up the enemy advance. The firing on both sides was very intensive and the air reverberated with deafening crashes of exploding shells. Suddenly, firing on both sides stopped dead and a silence fell. Looking over their barrier, the astonished British saw four or five wonderful beings much bigger than men between themselves and the Germans. They were white-robed and bareheaded, and seemed rather to float than stand. Their backs were toward the British, and they faced the Germans with outstretched arms and hands. The sun was shining quite brightly at the time. Next thing the British knew was that the Germans were retreating in great disorder.[19]

Two other British officers gave a similar report:

The British expected annihilation, as we were almost helpless, when to our amazement the Germans stood like dazed men, never so much as touched their guns, nor stirred till we had turned round and escaped by some crossroads. One man said he saw 'a troop of angels' between us and the enemy. He has been a changed man ever since. Another man was asked if he had heard the wonderful stories of angels. He said he had seen them himself. When he and his company were retreating, they heard the German cavalry tearing after them. They saw a place where they thought a stand might be made, with sure hope of safety, but, before they could reach it, the German cavalry were upon them. They therefore turned around and faced the enemy, expecting nothing but instant death, when to their wonder, they saw between them and the enemy, a whole troop of angels. The German horses turned round terrified and regularly stampeded. The men tugged at their bridles, while the poor beasts tore away in every direction from our men.[20]

Many of the German prisoners taken that day had surrendered when there was no need to do so. When interrogated, some of the prisoners described how they thought they were greatly out-numbered. It seems that the angels appeared to them as Allied reinforcements.[21] Other collaborated accounts of the intervention of angels in the retreat from Mons were reported by senior officers,[22] and these events provoke the question: 'Are there angel beings outside conventional time and space as we know it, that play a key role in managing the future?'

While researching 'angels' I heard an account by Mrs Joy Butler, a chaplain at the Sydney Adventist Hospital, a leading Australian medical institution. Joy and her husband had been working in Harare, Zimbabwe, for a number of years. On the day before they left to return to Australia in April 1993, Jo, a friend of Joy, rang to tell her of a remarkable incident which had just happened to a friend of hers.

Jo's friend had arrived home in her car with her five-year-old daughter. The mother stepped out of the car to open the front gate while leaving the engine running. A man who had been hiding behind the front hedge, jumped into the driver's seat and drove off with the daughter still in the back seat. The mother's screams and shouts caught the attention of another man who realised what had happened and set off in his car to give chase.

The distraught mother continued to scream and a man driving by stopped his car. He invited the mother to come with him to the police station. The poor mother was hesitant about this but when the man explained that he was a minister of religion and she saw a Bible on the front seat of his car, she agreed to accept his help. The man then prayed and asked God to let the car break down so that the pursuers could catch up. Apparently the mother had explained to the minister that the car had a full tank of fuel and could go a long way. These sort of 'car-jackings' were quite common in the city of Harare at that time and often the stolen cars were driven across the border to a neighbouring country where they were sold.

The mother and the minister set off in his car to give chase. They had not travelled far when they came upon the stolen car stopped on the road. The little girl was safe and the man had been caught. The little girl told her mother and the minister that she was pleading with the thief to take her back to mummy when she saw an angel appear on the bonnet of the car. The girl said the angel pushed what appeared to be a long shining sword down into the bonnet and the car stopped. When the car was inspected later it was found that the clutch had burnt out. Given that the woman was not aware of a mechanical problem and that the car had a full tank of petrol, it seems remarkable that the clutch could 'burn out' in such a short time.

While some readers may be sceptical about this story, I believe that a child's testimony in these circumstances is likely to be highly accurate. To write off such incidents is, in my view, to ignore important clues about the existence and nature of a reality outside conventional space-time. For example, it appears that angels have often revealed the future to people in dreams, and a number of these examples, some of which have changed the course of history, will be discussed in the next chapter.

Since the seventeenth century science has been seen as an important way of knowing the future in a limited sense. In the late 1600s Isaac Newton discovered the laws of motion and gravity. He showed that these laws govern not only the motion of objects on earth but also the motion of the planets in the solar system. On this basis he could not only predict simple matters like the time for a ball to fall from the top of a tower to the ground but also matters of greater complexity like the path of the planets and where they would be in the sky at any given time. Newton viewed the world as a vast perpetual-motion machine and the universe as a great uniform mathematical system. Thus, on the basis of mathematical calculation, scientists learned how to predict accurately a wide range of natural phenomena. Faith in the mechanical paradigm proved to be irresistible. Within two years of publishing his theories in *Philosophiae Naturalis Principia Mathematica* in 1687, some 18 editions were called for and by the end of the seventeenth century the foundations of modern science were firmly laid.[23]

Since that time our knowledge of the laws of nature have expanded to cover heat, light, sound, electricity, nuclear reactions, genetics and so forth. For example, we can predict what the temperature of a red-hot block of iron will be after it has cooled for an hour, or we can predict the characteristics of a plant that has been bred from certain parent stock. We are limited in our predictions to simple mechanical systems, however, where we know the mechanical laws governing those systems. That is, in a sense, the future is predestined because nature obeys these laws which constitute a sort of destiny field. Events progress towards their natural outcomes much like a ball falls towards the centre of the earth under the influence of the earth's gravitational field.

Similarly, through science we have learned about DNA—a giant molecule within the cells of everything that lives and which is responsible for programming the characteristics of the organism at each stage of development, from fertilisation to maturity, whether it be a giant redwood tree, a whale, or a human. Thus the development of a child is predestined within certain limits; that is, the colour of the hair, eyes, shape of face, skin type, and so forth, will form as predetermined unless external influences disrupt the genetic programming. We could therefore say that the future of the cell is stored in its genetic code, and every single cell in the organism contains that genetic code. For example, we could take off the tip of the leaf of a cauliflower plant and, using tissue culture, grow a complete new cauliflower plant.

This concept that in parts of nature the future is preordained, and that conventional space-time is governed by the laws of physics which in a sense constitute a destiny field, may provide important clues to an even bigger picture.

The predictive power of science is limited in many natural systems where there are an enormous number of possible interactions, such as in animal or insect populations, or in the human body, because the results of the interactions cannot be calculated. For this reason it can be very difficult to predict the long-term side effects of a new drug or food additive, because human biochemistry involves such a large number of reactions and thousands of different types of molecules. All the possible outcomes cannot be worked out and hence the overall outcome cannot be known.

Predicting the weather is an example where despite modern technology in the form of satellite weather pictures and powerful computers, we still cannot accurately know the future more than a day or so ahead. Even then the forecasts are often inaccurate in terms of detail. In the past, people had used patterns in nature to provide a way of predicting the weather. On the east coast of Australia farmers would notice the movement of black cockatoos and know that rain or a storm was likely to follow in a day or so.

In ancient times people believed that the destiny of humankind was in the hands of the gods and sought signs or omens in nature which might indicate their will.[24] Diviners—men and women skilled in the interpretation of signs and omens and foretelling the future—were especially sought after by kings before going into battle. This art of divining was well established in Babylon by the first millennium BC. Joan Oates, a specialist in Babylonian history and archaeology at the University of Cambridge, tells us that divination was a basic feature of Babylonian life. Senior practitioners were men of influence who were consulted on all important occasions. For example, the Babylonian army was always accompanied by a diviner whose job it was to look for omens in natural phenomena or to make contact with the gods.[25] The Babylonians placed particular emphasis on celestial portents which led to the development of astrology as a way of predicting the future. Astrology became an extension of the Babylonian religions and the leading astrologers were also priests.

By 419 BC the well-known signs of the zodiac were born and the practice soon followed of foretelling a person's future derived from a study of the relative positions of the sun, moon, planets and zodiac constellations at the time of a person's birth. The oldest known horoscope dates from 410 BC.[26]

The fascination with astrology spread to Greece, Rome, India and China. The belief in astrology continued on through the Christian era and the Middle Ages down to the present time. For example, John Dee chose an astrologically propitious day for the coronation of Queen Elizabeth I of England, and most Tudor monarchs and their advisers consulted astrologers and used their advice.[27] Billionaire J P Morgan, one of the greatest financiers in the United States whose financial empire underpinned banks, the US Steel Corporation and the famous White Star Line, owners of the *Titanic*, had his own personal astrologer. It is intriguing that Morgan cancelled his reservation on the ill-fated liner just before it sailed.[28]

According to a national survey in modern-day France, an estimated 50 per cent of men and 70 per cent of women read astrological columns in newspapers and magazines,[29] and the statistics for most western countries are likely to be similar. Professor George O Abell, Professor of Astronomy at the University of California, found in the United States at least 90 per cent of people consider themselves to be open minded about astrology with about 33 per cent having a firm belief in astrological predictions.[30]

Interestingly, recent scientific research has begun to lend support to certain astrological claims and, in particular, the relationship between the position of the planets at birth and the human personality. The main research in this field has been led by the French psychologist and statistician Michel Gauquelin, who has been accumulating statistical evidence for over 20 years. Gauquelin and his assistants contacted civil registries in thousands of towns and cities and obtained the birth records of more than 16 000 famous people. Analysis of the data gave a number of fascinating results.[31]

Among 3647 scientists and doctors, 724 instead of the 626 expected (that is, the calculated theoretical number on the basis of the theory of probability) were born after the planet Mars rose above the horizon or just after Mars reached its culmination or highest position in the sky. On the basis of calculation there is only a one in 500 000 possibility that the excess of scientists born under this birth sign was due to chance.

For 3438 well-known military men, Jupiter and Mars were more frequently found in their rise or culmination zones. For Jupiter there were 703 instead of the expected 590. The possibility of this being due to chance is less than one in a million.

When data for sports champions was examined, the correlation between birth times and the rise and culmination of the planet Mars associated with war and aggression was particularly strong. Among 2088 champion sportsmen, Mars was found to be rising or culminating 452 times rather than the expected 358 times. The probability of this happening by chance is calculated to be about one in five million.

On the other hand, Mars was much less likely to be found in the rising or culminating zones at the time of birth of famous painters, musicians and writers. Among the 2339 great painters and musicians studied, only 323 instead of the expected 402 were associated with the position of Mars. The probability of this being due to chance is less than one in 1000.

Gauquelin and his research team found that the results were constantly repeated from one country to another for similar professional groups, which further diminishes the possibility that the results were due to chance. Their work was reviewed by scientists from a variety of disciplines including astronomers, statisticians, demographers, gynaecologists and physicists and no alternative explanation for the results could be found.

The Belgian Committee for the Scientific Investigation of Alleged Paranormal Phenomena (PARA) followed up Gauquelin's research and repeated his experiments on a new group of 535 French and Belgian sports champions. The statistical analysis of the positions of Mars, as calculated by a computer programmed with accurate astronomical data, again showed a much greater frequency than expected for the rise or culmination of Mars at the time of birth of all these champions. When birth data for ordinary people was analysed the same phenomenon did not appear. The PARA committee noted these facts and considered that they posed a true scientific problem.[32]

Research was continued by Gauquelin and his co-workers, who studied the biographies of 570 French sports champions. Of these, 136 were born after the rising or culmination of Mars. The researchers found that when biographers were describing the character of these 136 people, they very frequently used words such as 'energetic, brave, wilful, hard-working, tireless, aggressive, exceptional temperament, quick to make decisions, resolute, great fighter, dynamic'. For sports champions born at hours when Mars was neither rising nor culminating, the above qualities were rarely described. While there were some obvious exceptions, when the data was analysed on the basis of probability, the temperamental differences between the Mars group and the non-Mars group were found to be absolutely decisive.[33]

Biographical data on other professional groups was also collected by Gauquelin. After analysis he was confronted with the curious finding that the planetary positions at birth seemed to be linked to certain personality traits and temperamental dispositions which were quite marked in the notable individuals studied.

Gauquelin's findings give support to the ancient intuition of astrology that a person's future achievements in life may be predicted with modest accuracy on the basis of his or her time of birth. His research did not totally support the traditional interpretations of astrology, however. While the planet Mars, symbol of the god of war, is dominant among military professionals, the planet Saturn, traditionally held as leading to a reflective life, appears for scientists and the Moon is frequent among poets, correlations for the other heavenly bodies were not evident from the statistics. The Sun does not appear among the leaders, be they political or military, nor Venus for musicians, painters or actors, nor Mercury for businessmen and writers. Jupiter, traditionally considered as a 'stable' planet is abnormally strong among the great Nazi dignitaries. It also appears that none of the more distant planets—that is, Uranus, Neptune and Pluto—fulfil the symbolism that modern astrologers have attributed to them.[34] Nonetheless, the strong correlations that have so far been observed provide evidence of a strange phenomenon which appears to be linked to a blueprint for the future.

Further evidence for such a blueprint comes from probability studies with tarot cards. Since about the fourteenth century tarot cards have been used by fortune-tellers to reveal the future. It is of course possible to read one's own cards and today many people practise tarot card reading as a way of life. One such practitioner was the physicist Dr Jane English, who became interested in reconciling, if possible, tarot with the mechanical worldview of physics in the 1980s. As a tarot practitioner she was in the habit of beginning each day by first meditating for about 20 minutes and then selecting a card from a face-downwards spread of a tarot deck. This first selection was a selection for body; that is, she was interested in getting a feeling from the tarot of the state of her body. She then made a second selection, this time for mind, then a third for spirit. She recorded these three selections each day in her diary.

When Dr English became interested in the comparison of tarot and physics, she had already recorded 1982 selections. The tarot contains 78 cards, so over the 1982 selections each card should have been drawn on average about 25 times. Certain cards were selected much more frequently than expected, however, as if the meditation process was influencing the selection of the cards. When she analysed her selections using the standard statistical tables used by scientists, the probability of her selection was only three chances in 10 000.

Moreover, Dr English had two friends who had kept similar diary records of their tarot readings. One had accumulated 2395 selections and had a probability of being due to chance of one in 10 000. The other had accumulated 2015 selections but had a calculated probability of being due to chance of less than one in 10 billion.

After analysing her tarot readings, Dr English carried out a 'control' test using a pack of cards which were blank on one side and numbered 1 to 78 on the other. She then made the same number of selections that she had recorded in her diary, 1982 in all, but this time the selections were made without meditation. When she analysed the results the probability of her selection was 47 per cent or approximately one in two. The control selection had been in accordance with that predicted by statistical tables and probability theory. Dr English's experience was later published in the book *The Wheel of Tarot: A New Revolution.*[35]

Professor Brian McCusker, Emeritus Professor of Physics at the University of Sydney, became aware of Dr English's research in the early 1980s and repeated the experiment, using two subjects who followed the same method. After meditation three selections were made and recorded for 365 days. The selections of one participant had a probability of occurring by chance of only about one in 100 000. The other participant had a probability of her 1095 selections occurring by chance of only one in a million billion billion (that is, one in 10^{24}).[36] This result could be seen to support the hypothesis that the selection of the tarot cards was somehow managed or supervised by an external mind which communicated with the subject through meditation.

Professor McCusker also carried out a control experiment where the same subjects each day selected a card from a deck of 52 playing cards. This selection was made under similar conditions to the tarot cards but without meditation. Again, as in Dr English's experiment, the control selection was in good agreement with probability theory, giving results that would be expected on a chance basis.

Post-nineteenth century science has traditionally dismissed stories of angels, answers to prayer or miracles, and premonitions and dreams that came true as imaginings of the mind or natural coincidences. Often the reliability of the observer is questioned or the accuracy of the interpretation of what they saw is doubted. The results of the tarot experiments strongly contradict the predictions of the Newtonian mechanical view of the universe, as do precognitive dreams and the Princeton University mind–machine experiments.

In the following chapters I will continue to look at the evidence that lies outside the mechanical worldview. I will review some of the dreams that have changed or foretold the course of history and examine premonitions and visions that accurately predicted the future. I will discuss in detail fascinating experiments conducted at Princeton University where certain subjects were able to see what another person was doing up to 30 hours or so ahead of time.

I will present some of the amazing examples in nature in which animals and insects can somehow know that they have to fly or migrate unguided to some destination where they have never been before. I will present evidence for the existence of destiny fields, demonstrated not only in the lives of animals but also in the history of this world. These examples, together with unusual phenomena noted by scientists, give support to a holographic model for existence where information about the past and future is always present, just as every part of a hologram contains information about the whole of the image it encodes.

I will explain how this model accounts for an eternity existing outside the conventional concept of time—an eternity which contains the past, present and future. I will then look at cycles of time and the principle of cycles approximating 1000 years or millennia. I will look at the most accurate calendar ever devised, that of the ancient Maya of Central America, which is more accurate than the one we currently use in the modern western world and which was used to predict the future on the basis of cycles of time.[37] I will explore other ancient traditions that suggest that we will soon enter the seventh millennium, which from the perspective of other historical visions of the future is to be a very special period in the history and future of the Earth.

In the final chapter I will discuss one of the most challenging puzzles that we face. If we can know the future and have free choice, can we change our individual future for the better? I believe we can, but to do so depends on our realisation that the future of this planet has already been mapped out and our choices are limited by the constraints of destiny fields already in place.

Chapter One

Dreams that Revealed the Future or Changed the Course of History

Records of dreams that foretold the future date from ancient times to the present. They form a fascinating tapestry which provides a basis for believing there is a non-material component of our existence. In this chapter I will carefully examine a number of dream experiences and discover the clues about the future which they provide.

Dr Robert Van de Castle, the former director of the Sleep and Dream Laboratory at the University of Virginia Medical School, has researched dreams for more than 30 years. He writes:

> Historians have generally ignored achievements originating from nocturnal inspiration ... Nevertheless, dreams have had a dramatic influence on almost every important aspect of our culture and history. Dream images have expanded our artistic, musical, and literary horizons, spurred generals to conquer empires, and led to inventions and industrial products that have revolutionised science and society.[1]

Many of us may not realise that dreams have played such an important part in shaping culture and the history of our world. Some dreams hint of an interaction with an external intelligence or mind that regulates the expansion of knowledge, the balance of political power and oversees the destiny of our planet.

Some of us may be surprised to learn that a dream expedited political freedom in India. The British rulers attempted to suppress any agitation that might lead to the liberation of India by imposing the harsh Rowlett Act of 1919. This legislation empowered the authorities to imprison without trial those suspected of sedition. At this time the young Indian lawyer Mohandas Karamchand Gandhi had been actively seeking ways to free his people from colonial subjugation. He later wrote that after weeks of meditation, he had a dream which suggested that the people of India suspend their usual business activities for 24 hours and devote that time to fasting and prayer.[2] The resulting non-violent mass strikes of 1919 which he organised marked a major turning point in India's efforts to achieve self-determination.[3]

Another event that changed the course of history and which involved a powerful dream or vision was the liberation of Rome from Maxentius in AD312 by Emperor Constantine I and his subsequent conversion to Christianity. When Constantine was contemplating his attack on Maxentius he experienced a waking vision of a Christian cross of light which bore the inscription 'Conquer by This'. That same evening, in a dream, Constantine had a vision of Christ who told him to have the insignia placed on the shields of his soldiers to safeguard against the enemy. Constantine ordered his soldiers to decorate their shields accordingly before the attack. Maxentius was subsequently defeated in a remarkable manner at the Milvian Bridge and was killed during the rout.[4]

Professor Arnold Jones, formerly Professor of Ancient History at Cambridge University, notes that the details of this vision were told later by Constantine I to his biographer Eusebius of Caesarea and confirmed under oath.[5] The dream was decisive in Constantine's conversion to Christianity and from AD313 onwards he regarded himself the chosen servant of the 'Highest Divinity'. Constantine ended the then widespread persecution of Christians and endorsed Christianity as the official religion of the far-flung Roman Empire.

In the decade following his conversion, Constantine's legislation

showed many signs of Christian influence and included the introduction of Sunday as the official public holiday for worship. During
the last decade of his reign, he became increasingly pious and
devoted more and more time to reading and studying the Christian
scriptures, listening to sermons and even delivering homilies to his
court.[6] These actions in his lifetime strongly testify that Constantine
experienced a dream that subsequently changed his life and affected
the lives of hundreds of millions of others. The stories of Gandhi
and Constantine both ask the question: 'Were these men fulfilling
a destiny which was facilitated through their dreams and managed
by an external mind?'

Dreams have also been responsible for some of the notable
advances in philosophy and science. One of the most influential
philosophers since the 1600s was the French mathematician Rene
Descartes. As a young man of 33 years, he experienced vivid
dreams on the evening of 10 November 1619. He wrote down
the dreams and puzzled over their interpretation for some time
until, eventually, from the first dream, he developed the philosophical theory of dualism. This asserted the separation of
humankind's mental and physical elements. Descartes' philosophy
was that a human's physical body functioned in a manner similar
to that of other animals, but that the mind of humans operated
on a non-physical basis under the influence of a soul. From
another dream he concluded that all the sciences could be
combined using mathematics. He then set about to combine
Euclidean geometry and algebra by inventing analytical geometry.
This led to the system of Cartesian co-ordinates, which are still
used as the basis of the construction and interpretation of graphs
of scientific data.[7] These new perspectives had a profound effect
upon the worlds of philosophy and mathematics and ultimately
led to the Cartesian or 'mechanical' worldview which forms the
basis of modern science.

A number of other mathematicians have reported receiving solutions to mathematical problems in dreams.[8] One outstanding example of this was the work of Indian mathematician Srinivasa Ramanujan, who contributed major advances to number theory in the early 1900s. According to a biographical article published in *Scientific American* in 1948, Ramanujan was favoured with help by a mathematical mentor in his dreams who showed him mathematical formulae that he would subsequently verify after waking. In his dreams his mentor was a goddess named Namakkal. This pattern of receiving mathematical formulae in his dreams repeated itself throughout his life.[9]

One of the most amazing facts regarding these dreams is that Ramanujan came from a poor family in India in the late nineteenth century and had only a limited education. He more or less taught himself mathematics and approached the subject in a very unconventional manner. Ramanujan's achievements were brought to the attention of Godfrey H Hardy at Trinity College, Cambridge University, one of the world's leading mathematicians at the time. Hardy was astonished and commented that he had never seen anything in the least like these mathematical formulae before: 'A single look at them is enough to show that they could only be written down by a mathematician of the highest class.' Hardy was able to prove some of Ramanujan's theorems only by deploying the full range of his considerable mathematical skills and then only with the greatest difficulty.[10]

Ramanujan's mysterious dreams again provide clues suggesting input from a knowing external mind, since to this day nobody understands how he could otherwise have worked out the theorems. Commenting on these remarkable feats, Paul Davies, Professor of Mathematical Physics at the University of Adelaide in South Australia, wrote:

It is very tempting to suppose that Ramanujan had a particular faculty that enabled him to view the mathematical Mindscape directly and vividly, and pluck out ready-made results at will.[11]

Important scientific discoveries and technological breakthroughs have also been made as a result of dreams. In 1869, Dmitri Ivanovich Medeleyev, Professor of Chemistry at the Technological Institute at St Petersburg, was working on a way to categorise the chemical elements based upon their atomic weights, but without success. One night, however, he received the solution to the problem while he slept. He later reported: 'I saw in a dream, a table where all the elements fell into place as required. Awakening, I immediately wrote it down on a piece of paper. Only in one place did a correction later seem necessary.'[12]

The result of this dream was the invention of the periodic table of elements, which is now used worldwide to teach chemistry. What is so amazing is that not enough elements were known at the time to fill all the spaces in the table which he saw in his dream. On the basis of these gaps, Medeleyev predicted the existence of three new elements which had not yet been discovered. His prophecy was proven within 15 years by the discovery and study of gallium in 1875, scandium in 1879 and germanium in 1886.

Another breakthrough discovery in chemistry was made as a result of a dream by the German chemist Friedrich August Kekule who, in the latter part of the nineteenth century, laid the ground-work for the modern theory of the structure of organic molecules. The tetravalent nature of carbon had been discovered by both Kekule and the Scottish chemist A S Couper in 1858. However, the problem of the structure of benzene with its six carbons but only six hydrogens, and the numerous ring compounds related to it, remained unsolved for several more years. In 1865, Kekule saw the solution to the puzzle in a dream. He had been attempting for some time to solve the structural riddle of the benzene molecule. He fell asleep in a chair and began to dream of atoms flitting before his eyes, forming various structures and patterns. Some long rows of atoms formed and began to twist in a snake-like fashion. Suddenly, one of the snakes seized hold of its own tail and began to swirl in a circle. Kekule awoke 'as if by a flash of lightning' and began to work out the implications of his dream imagery. He constructed a model of a closed ring with an atom of carbon and hydrogen at each point of a hexagon.[13] All the facts of organic chemistry known up to that time then fell into place.

Kekule later described his dream-discovered insight to a scientific convention in 1890 and concluded by urging the audience: 'Let us learn to dream gentlemen, and then we may perhaps find the truth.' When some scientists were asked to comment on Kekule's famous discovery they didn't hesitate to point out that his story presented 'a damaging picture of scientists' because scientists 'get hard facts' and 'don't dream things up'.[14]

Despite these protestations, however, substantial evidence has accumulated that dreams have provided ideas and information ahead of time. Another case in point occurred in 1921 when Frederick Banting was carrying out research into the cause of diabetes at the University of Toronto. He awakened from his sleep one night and wrote down these sentences: 'Tie up the duct of the pancreas of a dog. Wait for a few weeks until the glands shrivel up. Then cut it out, wash it out and filter the precipitation.' This new approach resulted in his successfully isolating the hormone now known as insulin, which is secreted in insufficient amounts, or not at all, in diabetics. The discovery, by Banting and his colleague C H Best, of a means of extracting this substance from non-human pancreases has since saved the lives of untold millions of diabetics.[15] Banting received the 1923 Nobel Prize in medicine for his dream-inspired discovery.

A very interesting example of precognitive inventive dreaming occurred in 1940. That spring, German forces were advancing through Belgium and France leading to the isolation of the British army at Dunkirk. In New York a young engineer by the name of D B Parkinson was working on a telephone project. He knew little about weapons and was designing a special potentiometer for an automatic level-recorder for civilian telephone use. One night he dreamt that he was among the beleaguered armies on the Continent and close to what looked to him like pieces of artillery equipment. He noticed the remarkable accuracy of one particular gun—every shell it fired brought down an enemy airplane. After a number of shots, one of the men in the artillery crew smiled at him and beckoned him to come closer to the gun. When he drew near, the gunner pointed to the exposed end of the left trunnion of the gun. Mounted there was the control potentiometer of the level recorder which he had been working on. Parkinson later said: 'There was no mistaking it. It was the identical item.'

When Parkinson told his dream to other staff, they saw the significance of it and acted quickly. From research based upon the dream, the Bell Laboratory developed the M9 gun director which is an analogue computer control for firing anti-aircraft guns. This device was used very successfully during the Second World War. In particular, in one week in August 1944 the German forces launched 91 buzz bombs towards England from the Antwerp area and the M9 directors destroyed 89 of them.[16]

This dream incident, which is recorded in a historical perspective titled *A History of Engineering and Science in the Bell System: National Service in War and Peace (1925–1975)* published by Bell Telephone Laboratories, may provide some important clues about our understanding of the origins of ideas and knowledge. Firstly, the young engineer knew very little about weapons and was not involved in or thinking about weapon development. Second, in the dream, even though he noticed the remarkable accuracy of the gun, his reaction was to marvel at this rather than inquire as to how it was achieved. He had actually to be 'beckoned' over to see the device in action and then to recognise his device in this strange situation before the idea 'clicked'. This sequence of events admits to the possible explanation that there was an external intelligence (mind) which could see the war situation as well as the application of electrical analogue technology. An entirely new application of the technology was communicated to the receptive mind using a dream. The device itself was one of several key inventions which contributed to the final outcome of the Second World War and thereby changed the course of history.

The examples we have just discussed reveal how new knowledge such as mathematical formulae, the periodicity of the chemical elements, chemical structures and engineering devices came about through revelations in dreams, as opposed to logical reasoning or experimental observations. A question we might now ask is whether or not these observations help explain the puzzle concerning the advanced knowledge of astronomy, geometry and engineering possessed by many ancient civilisations.

For example, it is well known that one of the big mysteries for archaeology has been the origin of the Egyptian pyramids. Writing about the enigma of the pyramids in his book *Fingerprints of the Gods*, researcher Graham Hancock states:

What is remarkable is that there are no traces of evolution from simple to sophisticated, and the same is true of mathematics, medicine, astronomy and architecture and of Egypt's amazingly rich and convoluted religio-mythological system . . .[17]

Did the Egyptians and other ancient peoples receive this knowledge that was so advanced, even by the standards of just last century, from an all-knowing mind, through dreams? We will probably never know for sure the answer to this puzzle, but as we consider the evidence for the past there may be clues about the puzzle of the future.

Let us consider the pyramids of ancient Egypt in more detail. The Great Pyramid at Giza built by Khufu (Cheops in the Greek form), was originally 146 metres high and measured 229 metres on each of its four sides. The construction was extraordinarily precise. The pyramid is accurately level and exactly square with no more than a 0.2-metre difference in length between the sides of the pyramid. The sides are aligned true north, south, east and west, indicating an advanced knowledge of astronomy and surveying.

The dimensions and geometry of the pyramid are such that if a circle is imagined where the centre is the top of the pyramid and the radius is the height of the pyramid, the circumference of that circle is exactly the circumference of the base of the pyramid, that is, the sum of the length of the four sides at the base. This feature suggests knowledge of the value of pi, centuries ahead of the Greeks.

The pyramid contains an estimated 2.3 million blocks of stone averaging 2.5 tonnes with the biggest stone weighing a massive 15 tonnes.[18] We do not know for sure how long it took to build the pyramids. The Greek historian Herodotus who lived in the fifth century BC records that Cheop's pyramid took 20 years to build. However, the Bent Pyramid of Dahshur, which was built by Cheops' father Seneferu (or Snofru), contains an inscription in the base referring to the twenty-first year of the king and, halfway up, another inscription referring to the twenty-second year. This implies that the pyramid took less than two years to build, which in a sense is reasonable, given that the king would not know how long he had to reign. (Some of the kings of the previous dynasty ruled for only a short time, such as Sekhemkhat and Khaba who ruled for eight years and four years respectively.)[19] Cheops ruled for 23 years. If we use a 20-year period for our example, we can calculate the rate at which the construction stones were put in place. On the assumption that the Egyptian builders worked 12 hours per day continuously for 20 years, the 2.3 million blocks would require 26.3 stones to be put in place each hour, or just over two minutes to place each block, averaging 2.5 tonnes accurately in place, tens of metres above the ground. Even if, say, 26 teams were placing almost one block an hour each, the co-ordination and precision required for this feat is truly amazing even by today's construction standards, and suggests a very highly developed knowledge of engineering. If we accept a shorter time period of just two years, in line with the dates given in the Bent Pyramid, we require that one of these huge stones was precisely placed every 13.5 seconds.

Contemporaneous with the building of these ancient pyramids was the ancient city of Ur in Sumer, which is now present-day Iraq. At this site lie the remains of a great ziggurat (a stepped pyramid-type building). The eminent archaeologist Sir Charles Leonard Woolley carried out major excavations at the site and later wrote that the diggings had revealed that at the time of the construction of the great pyramids of Egypt, the Sumerian architects were acquainted with the column, the arch, the vault and the dome; that is, all the basic forms of architecture. Referring to the ziggurat he goes on to say:

But the surprising thing is that there is not a single straight line in the structure. Each wall, from base to top and horizontally from corner to corner, is a convex curve, a curve so slight as not to be apparent but giving to the eye of the observer an illusion of strength where a straight line might have seemed to sag under the weight of the superstructure. The architect thus employed the principle of entasis, which was to be rediscovered by the builders of the Parthenon at Athens.[20]

(The Parthenon was built more than 1500 years later in the fifth century BC.)

Another ancient structure with advanced mathematical significance is Stonehenge in England, which dates to between 2000 and 1500 BC. Thirty blocks of grey sandstone, averaging 25 tonnes, stood in a circle about 30 metres in diameter. Professor Richard Atkinson, former Professor of Archaeology at University College in Cardiff, Wales, notes that some of the stones weigh up to 50 tonnes.[21] A stone of this weight will depress the ground upon which it is placed. Yet the builders of Stonehenge had somehow calculated how much the earth would be depressed when a large stone was put in place, so that it would still be perfectly aligned astronomically.

In 1963 Gerald S Hawkins, of the Smithsonian Astrophysical Observatory in the United States, calculated the directions of lines joining various stones at Stonehenge. He found that the monument may have served as an accurate astronomical calendar, capable of predicting the seasons of the year and even eclipses of the Sun and Moon. The positions of the huge stone slabs indicate the places on the horizon where the Sun and Moon rise and set at the summer and winter solstices; that is, at 21 June and 21 December each year. Using an advanced digital computer at the Massachusetts Institute of Technology, Hawkins found a remarkable correlation between the directions of these lines and the directions of the rising and setting of the Sun and Moon about 1500 BC. The chances of such correlations being coincidental have been calculated at about one in 100 million.[22]

The Mayan civilisation of Central America, which flourished from about AD250 to 800, also produced some remarkably accurate astronomical data. Not only were the vernal and autumnal equinoxes recorded with great accuracy, but the length of the solar day was measured to an accuracy of seven significant figures. The Mayans apparently kept the most accurate time the world has ever known.[23] Commenting on the accuracy of the Mayan calendar Hancock writes:

> In modern Western society we still make use of a solar calendar which was introduced in Europe in 1582 and is based on the best scientific knowledge then available: the famous Gregorian calendar ... Pope Gregory XIII's reform substituted a finer and more accurate calculation: 365.2425 days. Thanks to scientific advances since 1582 we know that the exact length of the solar year is 365.2422 days ... Strangely enough, though its origins are wrapped in the mists of antiquity far deeper than the sixteenth century, the Mayan calendar achieved even greater accuracy. It calculated the solar year at 365.2420 days, a minus error of only 0.0002 of a day.[24]

The instruments used by the Mayans to make these precise astronomical measurements have not been preserved or else have not yet been discovered. However, the isolated pockets of advanced mathematics, engineering and astronomy, from different parts of the ancient world manifest as remarkable scientific achievements by these ancient peoples. A possible explanation is that remnants of knowledge from an earlier unknown advanced race were somehow discovered or there was some sort of direct revelation such as Ramanujan experienced in his dreams.

Continuing with our study of the role of dreams in discovery, a baffling archaeological puzzle was solved as a result of an incredible dream that was later reported in the 1886 Proceedings of the Society for Psychical Research.

In 1893 Dr Herman Hilprecht, Professor of Assyrian Studies at the University of Pennsylvania, was studying fragments of agate found in the temple of Bel at Nippur. Working late one night, while attempting to decipher the inscription on two fragments of agate thought to be from Babylonian finger rings, he fell asleep shortly after midnight and had a dream that he recorded:

A tall, thin priest of the old pre-Christian Nippur, about forty years of age and clad in a simple abba, led me to the treasure chamber of the temple, on its southeast side. He went with me into a small, low-ceiled room without windows, in which there was a large wooden chest, while scraps of agate and lapis lazuli lay scattered on the floor. Here he addressed me as follows: 'The two fragments which you have published separately on pages 22 and 26 belong together, are not finger rings and their history is as follows: King Kuriglalzu (c. 1300 BC) once sent to the temple of Bel, among other articles of agate and lapis lazuli, an inscribed votive cylinder of agate. Then we priests suddenly received the command to make for the statue of the god of Ninib a pair of earrings of agate. We were in great dismay, since there was no agate as raw material at hand. In order to execute the command there was nothing for us to do but cut the votive cylinder into three parts, thus making three rings, each of which contained a portion of the original inscription. The first two rings served as earrings for the statue of the god; the two fragments which have given you so much trouble are portions of them. If you will put the two together you will have the confirmation of my word. But the third ring you have not found in the course of your excavations and you never will find it.'

With this the priest disappeared. After describing his dream Professor Hilprecht wrote:

I woke at once and immediately told my wife the dream that I might not forget it. Next morning—Sunday—I examined the fragments once more in the light of these disclosures, and to my astonishment found all the details of the dream precisely verified in so far as the means of verification were in my hands. The original inscription on the votive cylinder reads: 'To the god Ninib, son of Bel, his lord, has Kurigalzu, pontifex of Bel, presented this.'[25]

Commenting on this remarkable dream, Dr Robert Van de Castle notes that it raises some fascinating questions:

How did Hilprecht come to know that the fragments had been part of a single votive cylinder presented by King Kurigalzu, dedicated to Ninib, and subsequently made into a pair of earrings? What could account for the presence of these extraordinarily accurate details in the dream? Perhaps there was a psychic, or 'extrasensory', element involved. Perhaps logical, associative reasoning, assembling bits and pieces of subliminal information, is the explanation. If so, such superb deductive skill would put Sherlock Holmes to shame.[26]

As Van de Castle rightly asserts, it is hard to imagine that the human mind could have solved such a complex puzzle subliminally given the limited knowledge available—after all, his conscious mind had not supplied sufficient information to his brain beforehand. The dream does, however, demonstrate the possibility of a communication from an external mind, outside time and space as we know it, which knew the past.

In the preceding dream examples, it is fascinating that the new knowledge or clues are presented in a cultural context to which the dreamer can relate. For example, Ramanujan, who was of the Hindu faith, obtained knowledge from a Hindu goddess, while Hilprecht, an expert on ancient Assyrian history obtained knowledge from a priest from the pre-Christian period.

Some dreams that reveal the future contain similar cultural imagery rather than a photographic-type preview and some appear to contain a mixture of both. Prophetic dreams were well known to the ancients, and some of the oldest accounts were preserved in the extensive cuneiform library of the Assyrian King Assurbanipal II, ([669–626 BC], also known as Ashubanipal) which was found during the excavations of Nineveh in 1850. In one preserved dream account, Assurbanipal apparently was worried about an imminent battle against Elamite invaders. One of his priests reported having a dream in which the goddess Ishtar appeared with a quiver on either shoulder and a bow in her hand. She indicated that Assurbanipal should eat and drink and enjoy music because she would ensure victory the next day. In another account of the incident, Ishtar also appeared in the dreams of members of Assurbanipal's army and promised them victory. Victory did follow and a magnificently preserved series of large engraved panels in the British Museum graphically detail the defeat of the Elamites.[27]

Perhaps one of the oldest prophetic dream accounts involves the famous story of Joseph which is found in the ancient Hebrew book Genesis, believed to have been written about 1500 BC. This is a religious book and contains the well-known Creation and Noah's Flood stories, and many modern scholars are cautious about using it as an historical source. However, an increasing proportion of its historical content has been confirmed by recent archaeological discoveries, such as those of Professor Manfred Bietak of the Austrian Archaeological Institute in Cairo.[28]

Professor Harold Rowley, who was Professor of Hebrew Language and Literature at Manchester University, noted in his article on Genesis for the *Encyclopaedia Britannica*:

Excavations at Mesopotamian sites, and especially at Nuzi, have contributed much to bring about the greater respect for these stories that has come to be general. Customs which figure in these stories but which were obsolete at the time when the stories are believed to have been written down are known to have prevailed in the second millennium BC.

Professor Rowley goes on to comment:

The story of Joseph may reasonably be held to preserve more reliable historical memories. There is clear evidence of acquaintance with Egyptian life and customs ... Joseph's immovable integrity in prosperity or adversity and his magnanimity toward his brothers make this one of the great stories of the world, and there is no reason to doubt that it rests on actual history.[29]

The story of Joseph involves a number of prophetic dreams experienced by several different people. I will recount this famous story in detail because it provides significant insight into an apparent connection between dreams and destiny fields.

Joseph lived about 1900 BC in Canaan (present-day Palestine) and was one of the 12 sons of Israel (also known as Jacob), whose descendants became the ancient nation of Israel. When Joseph was about 17 years old he had a vivid dream in which he saw himself and his brothers binding sheaves in the field when, suddenly, his sheaf arose and stood upright while the other sheaves gathered around it and bowed down to Joseph's sheaf. When Joseph told the dream to his brothers, they were quick to interpret the dream as

Joseph telling them that he would one day rule over them all. This did not go down well with his brothers because Joseph, at this time, was the youngest of the 11 sons. (The twelfth brother was born later.) Joseph then reported another dream to his father and brothers. In this dream the Sun, the Moon and 11 stars were bowing down to him. His father, Jacob, saw that this dream implied that Joseph's father and mother as well as his brothers would one day bow down to him and rebuked his son for his story.

The dreams served to kindle the jealousy of Joseph's brothers to the point where they plotted to kill him so that his dreams could not come true. However, through the intervention of his eldest brother, Reuben, Joseph was instead sold to traders who were travelling to Egypt. Joseph's brothers took his robe, which had been especially made for him by his father and dipped it in goat's blood. When Jacob was shown the coat he immediately concluded that his youngest son had been killed by a wild beast.

In Egypt, Joseph was bought as a slave by the captain of the personal guard of the Pharaoh. The Genesis account tells that Joseph proved to be so capable and dependable that the captain made him overseer of his house. Joseph's career turned sour, however, when the young man refused the advances of the captain's wife and she then reported him to her husband for attempted rape. As a result, Joseph was imprisoned. His integrity and trustworthiness were also recognised by the gaoler and before long he was put in charge of the other prisoners. Later, the Pharaoh's chief butler and chief baker were imprisoned for offending him.

One night both servants had unusual and vivid dreams which they felt had special significance for their lives. They shared their dreams with Joseph, who at that time was responsible for their care. The butler dreamt there was a grapevine before him with three branches. As soon as it budded, blossoms shot forth and clusters ripened into grapes. The Pharaoh's cup was in his hand, and he filled the cup with juice from the pressed grapes and placed it in the Pharaoh's hand. Joseph interpreted the dream to the butler as revealing the future. In three days, represented by the three branches, he would be restored to his former position and once again pour wine into the Pharaoh's cup. The baker then told Joseph his dream. He saw himself carrying three cake baskets on his head. The upper basket was filled with special food for the Pharaoh but the birds were eating out of that basket. Joseph's interpretation of this dream was that the three baskets represented three days and that within that time the baker would be hung on a tree and birds would pick at his flesh.

The Pharaoh's birthday was in three days time, and on that day he reinstated the butler and hanged the baker.

Two years later the Pharaoh himself had a series of vivid dreams that troubled him greatly. Furthermore, his magicians and counsellors could not interpret the dreams. The butler then remembered Joseph, who was still in prison, and told the Pharaoh about this man who had correctly interpreted his dream and that of the baker. Joseph was brought before the Pharaoh who recounted to him the following two dreams. In the first dream he was standing on the bank of the River Nile when seven fat sleek cows came up out of the river and fed on the reeds. Then seven very gaunt cows came up and ate the first seven cows. In the second dream, seven full ears of grain were growing on one stalk and seven withered, thin and blighted ears sprouted after them and swallowed up the seven full ears.

After listening to the accounts, Joseph told the Pharaoh that he believed that the God of heaven was revealing the future to him. The seven fat cows and the seven full ears of grain indicated seven years of plenty, while the seven thin cows and the withered ears of grain that swallowed up the others were seven years of famine which would follow, consuming the existing resources. Joseph advised the Pharaoh that because the dream was doubled the future was fixed and that what the dreams revealed would shortly occur. He recommended that 20 per cent of all the harvest of Egypt over the seven plentiful years be stored away for food for the seven years of famine that would follow. This suggestion pleased the Pharaoh, who decided to appoint Joseph to oversee its operation.[30]

The Genesis account tells of how seven years of abundant harvest did follow and then a severe famine set in, presumably because of drought. Nearby Palestine was also affected and Joseph's brothers were sent by their father from Canaan to buy grain. Being foreigners in Egypt they had to appear before Joseph, where they paid obeisance to him and begged to buy food. Joseph's original dream was thereby fulfilled.

Through a series of events the rest of Joseph's family, including his father Jacob, came to Egypt as Joseph's guests, apparently fulfilling the prediction of his other dream (although there is no record of his parents bowing before him). Thus the Israelites came to Egypt where they lived for the next four centuries until their exodus under Moses.

While we have no way now of verifying the dream account, we have every reason to believe that the story is based on actual historical events as discussed earlier. The dream accounts in Joseph's story use agricultural imagery which was part of the family's everyday cultural experience, rather than a direct precognitive view or snapshot of the future. The difference between everyday cultural experience and a direct precognitive view may be an important clue to the nature of the future and the existence of destiny fields.

The initial duplicate dreams of Joseph indicated a noble future for him. His jealous brothers determined to prove his prophecy wrong by killing him. Their plans were interrupted by Reuben who planned to return Joseph to his father, but his plans, in turn, were thwarted by the unexpected arrival of traders travelling to Egypt, and a spur-of-the-moment decision by the other brothers to sell Joseph to them. The synchronicity of the events suggests the possibility of a destiny field influence. When Joseph was later accused of the attempted rape, his life was spared and he was imprisoned instead of killed. Here we see Joseph's life spared a second time. The events involving the butler and baker which raised him from obscurity to recognition by the most powerful ruler in the world at just the right time, also lends credence to a destiny field interpretation.

Some readers may doubt the reliability of the Genesis record. However, other authorities report similar accounts in their histories. The Greek historian Herodotus (c. 484–425 BC), tells of a dream had by the great Persian King Cyrus II. It was Cyrus who captured Babylon and brought its empire to an end and founded the Persian empire in its place. Using a clever military strategy, he diverted the River Euphrates from its course through the city. This enabled his general, Gobryas, to march troops along the riverbed and under the city's walls, thereby capturing it by surprise while the Babylonian king and city officials were partying.

Herodotus records a dream Cyrus had just before he was killed. Cyrus had crossed into the enemy territory of the Massagetae to conquer them. On the first night he dreamt that he saw a young man by the name of Darius with wings on his shoulders, shadowing Asia with one wing and Europe with the other. Darius was the 20-year-old son of Cyrus's ally Hystaspes, and Cyrus interpreted the dream to mean that Darius was plotting to take his crown and succeed him on the throne. Cyrus called for Hystaspes and sent him back to Darius in Persia with a warning. He then continued with his military campaign. Herodotus commented on the warning Cyrus gave to Hystaspes:

Thus Cyrus spoke, in the belief that he was plotted against by

Darius; but he missed the true meaning of the dream, which was sent by God to forewarn him, that he was to die then and there, and that his kingdom was to fall at last to Darius.[31]

Meanwhile Cyrus with his best troops, a day or two later, surprised a detachment of the Massagetae army. Many troops were slaughtered and a multitude taken prisoner, including the son of the Queen whose name was Tomyris. Tomyris sent to Cyrus for the release of her son. When Cyrus ignored her request she collected all the forces of her kingdom and attacked Cyrus. Herodotus reports that the greater part of the army of Persians was destroyed and Cyrus himself fell in the fighting.[32] Eight years later, after the death of Cyrus' son Cambyses II, in 522 BC, Darius did take over the mighty Medo-Persian empire, as the dream had foretold.

Herodotus also records an example of a clearly precognitive dream, as opposed to a prophetic dream using cultural symbols that requires interpretation. Herodotus at one stage lived on the Greek island of Samos in the Aegean Sea, just off the coast of Turkey. Seventy years earlier, the island had reached its height of prosperity under a despot named Polycrates who, by insurrection, had made himself master of the island. Herodotus tells how in 522 BC Oroetes, the Persian governor of Sardis, lured Polycrates to the mainland with a report of enormous gold and treasure. On the eve of Polycrates' departure, his daughter experienced a dream in which she saw her father hanging high in the air and the rain falling on his body. She was so distressed by her dream that she used every effort to prevent her father from going, even crying after him as he went on board his ship. Notwithstanding the many warnings previously given him by soothsayers, Polycrates ignored the pleas of his daughter and set sail for Magnesia. Upon arrival he was slain by Oroetes who hung his dead body on a cross. Herodotus wrote: 'Then was the dream of the daughter of Polycrates fulfilled; for

Polycrates, as he hung upon the cross, and rain fell on him, was washed by Jupiter.'[33]

It is interesting that despite the warnings of many soothsayers, and of friends who probably saw the risk of leaving the safety of the island, and despite his daughter's dream, Polycrates felt somehow compelled to go and was blind to the danger. These reactions suggest that at times we may experience some sort of destiny field which affects our reactions in much the same way that animals and insects are driven by some instinct to migrate.

An almost identical precognitive dream situation occurred before the assassination of Julius Caesar. It was recorded by the Roman historian Suetonius in the early part of the second century AD. He writes that the evening before the murder, Caesar's wife, Calpurnia, experienced a disturbing dream in which she saw herself holding her bleeding husband in her arms. She saw the dream as being prophetic and pleaded with her husband to stay home. The soothsayer Spurinna had also warned Caesar that danger would befall him before the Ides of March (15 March), and for these reasons Caesar hesitated for a long time over whether to stay home and delay what he had planned to do in the Senate. However, one of the conspirators, Decimus Brutus, urged Julius not to disappoint the full meeting that was waiting for him. On the way to the Forum a note revealing the plot was handed to Caesar but he did not read it immediately. When he took his seat, the conspirators gathered about him and stabbed him with their daggers.[34] As with Polycrates, Caesar ignored all the warnings, including the pleas of the woman who loved him, and also, as though under the influence of a destiny field, chose not to open the note which would have disclosed the plot.

In the famous play *Julius Caesar*, Shakespeare shows great insight about dreams. When Caesar describes his wife's dream to Decimus Brutus, the conspirator counters with the explanation that the dream required a different interpretation:

This dream is all amiss interpreted,
It was a vision fair and fortunate,
Your statue spouting blood in many pipes,
In which so many smiling Romans bathe'd,
Signifies that from you great Rome shall suck
Reviving blood, and that great men shall press
For tinctures, stains, relics and cognizance.
This by Calpurnia's dream is signified.[35]

In this passage, Shakespeare portrays Decimus Brutus as changing Calpurnia's experience from a precognitive prophetic dream to a symbolic prophetic dream, thereby making the interpretation more subjective and cunningly allaying Caesar's fears. Both Polycrates' and Caesar's deaths were planned assassinations and the number of assassinations down through history that were seen in detail beforehand in precognitive dreams is impressive.

Three days before his assassination in 1589, Henry III of France dreamed that all the royal vestments, the royal tunics and the orb and sceptre were bloodied and trampled underfoot by monks.[36] On 1 August, Jacques Clement, a Jacobin friar, gained admission to the King's presence and fatally stabbed him in the abdomen. He died in the early hours of the next morning.

A vividly detailed assassination dream was reported by the Englishman John Williams on 3 May 1812. He dreamt that he was in the lobby of the House of Commons and observed a small man enter in a blue coat and white waistcoat. He then saw a man in a tobacco-coloured coat with metal buttons fire a pistol, and a large bloodstain appear on the left breast of the small man's waistcoat before he fell to the ground. As the assassin was grabbed by several men nearby, the dreamer sought the victim's identity and was informed that it was Mr Perceval, the Chancellor of the Exchequer.

Williams awoke and told the dream to his wife but she advised him to disregard it. He had the dream a second time and again his wife told him it was just a dream and to forget it. Williams experienced the same dream a third time that night and became agitated.

Over the next day or so, he consulted with several friends as to whether he should try to alert someone in authority, but was strongly advised not to, lest he be ridiculed and considered a fanatic. Spencer Perceval, the then Prime Minister of England, was assassinated by a madman about a week later on 11 May 1812. The details of the assassination, including the colours of the clothing, the buttons on the assassin's jacket and the location of the bloodstain on Perceval's white waistcoat, were identical to those Williams said had appeared in his dream.[37]

A similar assassination dream from the perspective of an interactive observer was experienced by President Abraham Lincoln, about two weeks before his death. Lincoln dreamed that he heard subdued sobs, as if a number of people were weeping. Curious about the origin of these sobs, he left his bed and wandered downstairs from room to room, continuing to hear the same mournful sounds as he walked along. When he arrived at the East Room, he saw a coffin lying on a platform. The corpse was wrapped in funeral robes. Soldiers were stationed as guards around the coffin, which was surrounded by a throng of people. The face of the corpse was covered and when Lincoln demanded of one of the soldiers, 'Who is dead in the White House?' the soldier replied, 'The President. He was killed by an assassin!' The loud burst of grief from the crowd, when they heard this, woke Lincoln from his dream.

On the evening of Good Friday 1865, Lincoln was fatally shot by John Wilkes Booth as he sat in Ford's theatre in Washington. He died early the next morning, the 15 April. His casket was placed on a platform in the East Room of the White House, where it was guarded by soldiers.[38]

The assassination of Archduke Franz Ferdinand of Austria, which precipitated the First World War, was also clearly seen before it took place in a dream by Bishop Joseph Lanyi of Grosswardein in Hungary. Early on the morning of 28 June 1914, the bishop, who had been a former tutor to the archduke, had a dream in which he saw himself go to his desk and look through some letters. On the top of the pile of envelopes was a black-bordered letter bearing a black seal with the coat of arms of the archduke. The bishop opened the letter and on the upper part was a light blue post-card-like picture which showed a street scene. The archduke and his wife were sitting in a motorcar with a general facing them and another officer sitting next to the chauffeur. As a crowd assembled on both sides of the street, two young men suddenly jumped out and fired at the archduke and his wife. Below the picture the bishop read:

Dear Dr Lanyi,
    I herewith inform you that today, my wife and I will fall victims to an assassination. We commend ourselves to your pious prayers.

Kindest regards from your
Archduke Franz,
Sarajevo, the 28th of June,
3:45 A.M.

Awaking from his dream, the bishop immediately looked at the clock and noted that it was the same time as in the dream, 3.45 am. He went straightaway to his desk and wrote down everything that he had seen and read in his dream. A little later he drew a sketch of the assassination scene, had it witnessed by two people staying at his home and then sent the account to his brother Edward who was a Jesuit priest.

Later that day the archduke and his wife were murdered at Sarajevo by the Serbian student Gavrilo Princip. The bishop's drawings were in close agreement with photographs published in the press several days later, except that there had been only one assassin rather than the two in the bishop's dream.[39]

Dream researcher Dr Robert Van de Castle notes in relation to this dream experience that questions have been raised as to whether the bishop was really so thorough in recording all the events on that fateful day. However, subsequent questioning by journalists and editors of the two witnesses who signed the sketch and of the bishop's brother confirmed the dream story.[40]

Many other forms of personal tragedies have been foretold in dreams and visions. The international speaker Corrie Ten Boom, whose family hid Jews from the Nazis during the occupation of Holland in the Second World War saw the capture of herself and her family in clear detail four years before it actually happened.

On 10 May 1940, Corrie heard in the distance the first German bombs falling on Holland. While saying her prayers that day she experienced a clear vision or dream in her mind. She was looking at the town square where four enormous black horses were pulling a farm wagon. In the wagon was Corrie herself, her father and her sister Betsie. The wagon was crowded and further back she saw her sister Nollie and other relatives. None of them could get off the wagon and they were being taken somewhere.

Corrie wondered what the vision could mean, as it was many months before her family became involved in hiding Jews. On 28 February 1944, the hiding place was discovered by the Gestapo and the family together with their Jewish guests were taken to the police station for questioning. The next day Corrie, her father, sisters and the same relatives she had seen in her earlier vision were marched out to a green bus which then took them across the town square. They were being taken away against their will, just as she had seen nearly four years earlier.[41] The story of Corrie Ten Boom and her survival in the Nazi concentration camps was later made into the film *The Hiding Place*.

One of the saddest precognitive dream accounts I have read was reported by the mother of a little girl who died in the Aberfan mine disaster in Wales. Eryl Mai Jones had told her mother of a particular dream where 'We go to school but there is no school there; something black has come down all over it'. The little girl continued, 'I'm not afraid to die, Mommie. I'll be with Peter and June.' Two days later on 21 October 1966, a massive coal waste dump slid down the mountainside and engulfed the Welsh mining village of Aberfan, killing 144 people. Eryl Mai, Peter and June were among the 118 children crushed or buried alive.[42]

While the majority of precognitive dreams are related to tragedy or death, some dreams of the future have stimulated actions which have led to very pleasing outcomes. Sir Thomas White, a wealthy alderman living in London in the sixteenth century, dreamed that he founded a college at a place where three elm trees grew from one root. Some time later, when White was walking by a convent in Oxford, he was amazed to discover an elm with three trunks growing from the same root. He purchased the land the tree grew on and, in 1555, founded St John's College of Oxford University.[43]

Before the American Civil War, Harriet Tubman, a runaway slave from the South, led hundreds of other slaves to freedom in Canada using a network of escape routes which became known as the 'Underground Railroad'. Tubman made 19 rescue trips to the South to lead about 300 people to safety with slave-hunting patrols vigorously pursuing her. She claimed that she was shown safe pathways in her dreams. During all the trips she made, she never lost a single 'passenger'.[44]

The vast oilfield in the Burgan area of Kuwait was discovered as the result of a dream experienced in 1937 by Lieutenant Colonel H R P Dickson, a British political official. Dickson, who was in Kuwait at the time, experienced a strange dream involving a lone palm tree. He dreamed that next to this tree was a hole in the ground. He approached the hole and saw a sarcophagus at the bottom. Inside he discovered a shroud, and when he touched the shroud a beautiful maiden rose to life. Perplexed by his dream he consulted a local Bedouin woman who had a reputation as a dream interpreter. At that time, a British oil company crew had been unsuccessfully drilling for two years in the Bahrain area on Kuwait Bay. The Bedouin woman told Dickson that his dream foretold great wealth lying beneath the sands of Kuwait. He should move the drilling team to the desert of Burgan and concentrate drilling activities by a lonely palm tree, where they would find great treasure. When the drillers laughed at Dickson's urgings to move the team, he travelled to London and told his dream and its interpretation to the company executives. One of them believed in dreams and felt the dream interpreter's instructions deserved a try. He cabled Kuwait and the team was moved about 50 kilometres south to Burgan. Shortly afterwards, in May 1938, huge oil deposits were discovered in the desert beside a lonely palm tree.[45]

Another dream led to the discovery of treasure in the famous story of the fifteenth-century English tinker John Chapman. Chapman, who lived at Swaffham in Norfolk County, dreamed that if he journeyed to London and placed himself at a certain spot on London Bridge, he would meet someone who would tell him something of great importance regarding his future affairs. Chapman had the same dream three nights in a row and decided to make the trip to London. For three consecutive days he stood at the spot on the bridge that he saw in his dream. Towards evening on the third day, as he was beginning to doubt the significance of his dream, a stranger came up to him and asked why he had been standing at the same spot for so long. Without saying where he came from, the tinker told him about his dream. The stranger suggested that he return home and pay no more attention to dreams. To emphasise how silly dreams were, the stranger told him that he had recently dreamed that if he went to a place called Swaffham and dug under an apple tree in a certain garden on the north side of town, he would find a box of money.

The tinker immediately recognised the significance of the stranger's statement and returned home to Swaffham. Digging at the spot he thought had been indicated by the stranger, his spade struck something hard, which turned out to be an iron chest. He carried it home and found it was full of money. Engraved on the lid of the box was a Latin inscription which read, 'Under me both lye another much richer than I'. Digging deeper in the hole, the tinker found an even larger treasure chest, full of gold and silver coins.

Whether this is an embellished fifteenth-century folktale or a precognitive dream experience that actually happened is best reserved for the judgement of the reader. Whatever actually happened, Chapman's dream achieved fame because he showed his gratitude by donating a sizeable sum of money to the construction of a church in his home town in 1454. Pew carvings and stained-glass windows depicting the tinker can still be seen today in the Church of St Peter and St Paul.[46]

Possibly the largest collection of anecdotal precognitive dreams was collected by Dr Louisa Rhine, the wife of Dr J B Rhine who was director of a famous parapsychology laboratory at Duke University in the United States. More than 3000 accounts of pre-cognitive dreams were sent to her in response to appeals published in various popular media. Many of these dreams are discussed in her book, *Hidden Channels of the Mind*.[47] Her files include about 430 precognitive dreams dealing with events that could have been altered if the dreamer had taken steps to do so, but such an effort was made in only 30 per cent of these cases.

Dr Van de Castle notes that death seems to be the most prominent theme in precognitive dreams. Women outnumber men nearly two to one as dream receivers and close blood ties are involved in about 50 per cent of cases, although spouses and personal friends are also frequently involved.[48]

While researching this chapter I asked about 80 friends and acquaintances if they knew of anyone who had experienced a precognitive dream. In response, I learned of the following three accounts.

The first account was told to me by a research technician called Paul, who is employed in the food technology department of the research organisation where I work. One night in 1986 Paul, then a high school student, had a particularly vivid dream. He saw himself walking alongside his twin brother Stephen, who was on a stretcher being wheeled down a corridor past the school auditorium. Paul looked up and saw a physical education class in progress. One of the girls in the class recognised Paul, and smiled and waved her hand. Some months later Stephen received serious head injuries during a metalwork class. Paul, who was in the same class, remained with Stephen until ambulance officers arrived. Then he walked alongside the stretcher as his brother was wheeled to the ambulance. As they passed the auditorium, Paul looked up and realised he was seeing the same scene as in his dream. At that moment, the same girl Paul had seen in his dream, smiled and waved.

Paul commented to me that he has never forgotten the experience because the dream was so specific. The girl, the way she looked up, smiled and waved and the activities of the other students were exactly as he had seen in his dream months beforehand.

In another account a young woman described to me how in 1981 her father, while working in New Guinea, had a dream where he saw an angel showing him the book of his life. He noticed that each page represented a year and that there were only a few pages remaining. When he woke up he could not remember exactly how many pages were left in the book. He decided to write to each of his children, telling them how much he loved them, and he also took out a life insurance policy. In 1990, while back in Australia, he had the same dream again. This time he confided to his wife that the book was on the last page. Soon afterwards he went to a Pacific island to help with an aid program and was killed in a building construction accident.

The third account was a dream experienced by Joe Irwin, a member of staff in the engineering department of the research organisation where I work. He told me that when he was 18 years old and living near Mullumbimby, in New South Wales, he had an unusually vivid dream. It was different from the other dreams he had and he still remembers it clearly even though the incident occurred 10 years ago.

He dreamed that he was out in the surf on his surfboard when suddenly someone yelled 'Shark!'. Everyone in the surf quickly got out of the water. That part of the dream ended abruptly and he dreamed that he was now standing on the bank of a river. On either side of him stood people that he recognised from the church he attended. Suddenly part of the bank gave way and a girl to the left of him slipped and fell into the water, disappearing out of sight. Then, almost immediately, he saw the girl being pulled out of the river on the opposite bank by a bearded man wearing a white robe. The man's face was not distinguishable but he could see the girl's face clearly. She was no longer wearing her original clothes but was wearing a white robe the same as the man. The girl gave a cheery smile and a wave and then walked away with the man. Meanwhile, on his side of the river, everyone was crying because the girl had slipped under the water and they could not see her any more. It was as if they could not see the other side where she was pulled out. There the dream ended.

Joe told me that a couple of days later he went for a surf before going to church. Sharks were often seen on the northern New South Wales coast where he lived, but this time while he was surfing he saw two shark fins surface a mere six to eight metres away. Without hesitating, he and another older surfer nearby hastily paddled for the shore. Later that day when he went to church he learned from tearful friends of a terrible tragedy. The girl he had seen in his dream had been killed in a freak car accident during a storm the night before. That dream experience changed the direction of his life and he began to take his religious faith much more seriously.

These three accounts of precognitive dreams fit the characteristics commonly observed by Dr Louisa Rhine, and like Mike Martin's dream, provide convincing evidence that the human mind can communicate with and 'see' the future. Dr Van de Castle believes that 'Dreams have also given us a basis for believing that there is a non material component to our existence . . .'[49]

In this chapter we have reviewed dreams that foretold major events which have charted the history of the world. The assassination or death of important kings and leaders; the outcomes of major battles; warnings of famines and natural disasters; discoveries which advanced science, mathematics and medicine; the finding of one of the world's largest oil fields; the founding of one of the most prestigious university colleges; and the liberation of nations such as India, have all been foreseen in dreams. These examples are a mere fraction of the dream literature available.

In some instances, these precognitive or prophetic dreams were heeded and in some instances they were ignored, and yet the reactions of the people involved somehow played a part in fulfilling the destiny of the dream. For example, Polycrates ignored the desperate and public pleas of his daughter, even as he boarded his ship. If he had heeded the pleas and the advice of friends, would his mutilated body have swung in the rain as his daughter foresaw? His determination seems to indicate that he was under the influence of a strong compulsion or destiny field that blinded him to the danger and thereby ensured that the preordained future or destiny did occur.

Similarly with Caesar. The dream of his wife, the warnings of the soothsayer and his poor health at the time led him to hesitate and delay going to the forum. This had the potential to change the future from that foreseen by Calpurnia in her dream. However, again we have a set of circumstances which seem to ensure that the destiny is fulfilled. Decimus Brutus arrived and provided the pressure that helped Caesar decide to go, and then, on the way, Caesar again chose to ignore a warning that could have saved his life. His choice, which sealed his fate, suggests that many of the supposedly free choices that we make may in actual fact not be free but, rather, influenced by the unseen forces of destiny.

The decision to act on a dream or in accordance with a dream also seems to admit of a pressure from a destiny field to fulfil a future plan. The finding of the oil in Kuwait, the development of the M9 gun director, the founding of St John's College at Oxford and the finding of treasure by the tinker are examples of fulfilment of a future that one would not have expected without the dream of the future playing the key motivating role. On the other hand, what of the dreams of the future where the dreamer has not believed, has not acted, has not found the oil wells or treasure, and as a consequence has 'changed' the future from that which was revealed in the dream? How fixed is the future? How strong are the destiny fields?

Other prophetic and precognitive dreams seem to be mere chance communication between the human mind and some external mind which *sees* the future, or else some form of direct observation of a future which somehow *already exists*. It seems that certain events, especially tragic events such as the Aberfan mine disaster or wars, or planned assassinations and deaths of family members, generate particularly strong destiny fields, and that under these conditions communication between the future and the human mind takes place.

In the next chapter we will explore the concept of destiny pressure as experienced in the form of premonitions and prophecies. I will look at some of the ways that we can know the future apart from dreams. I will also look at the evidence that the future may be fixed in outline only and that the fine detail is filled in by our choices, as we get closer to the event.

Chapter Two

Prophecies and Predictions

One of the difficulties we have in comprehending the possibility of predicting or knowing the future relates to the almost infinite number of factors that affect any course of action or event. Every day we make thousands of choices, many of them subconsciously, yet those choices can have significant or profound effects on our lives.

For example, let us suppose we have stopped in a line of cars waiting to turn right at a set of traffic lights. The four cars in front of us move off after the lights turn green but as we let our clutch out we do not have quite enough revs on the engine, and our car stalls. We quickly restart the car, let out the clutch more carefully and move off. Just then the lights change to red and we have to stop, as do the three frustrated drivers behind us. We are now two minutes behind our planned schedule. The synchronicity of all near future events has also been changed by two minutes. This can have profound consequences. Half a minute after the lights changed the first time there may have been a traffic accident which the cars ahead of us were involved in but which we and the cars behind us have now missed. The driver behind us may now be feeling frustrated at having to wait the extra time. When we get through the traffic lights he may choose to drive faster than the speed limit in order to make up the time he had lost. This in turn may lead him to be booked by a policeman who is now on that particular stretch of road. As a result of this hold-up, the driver may miss the train he was trying to catch to a job interview. Because he was late he may have missed out on getting the new job, which may mean he can no longer change career. As a result his life may take a totally different course from that which would have occurred had he got this new job, all because of a total stranger accidentally stalling a car in front of him.

Alternatively, instead of speeding, the impatient driver behind us may, have chosen to overtake unsafely and as a result had an accident which changed the lives of another family. On the other hand, the driver behind us may have driven normally and arrived at the train station just as someone pulled out of a convenient parking space which saved him a two minute walk. More than likely, however, we might simply catch up with the four cars ahead at the next set of traffic lights and synchronicity is restored.

From this example, we can see that the possible scenarios are endless. The simple event of accidentally stalling a car can alter the coincidence of events and lead to vastly different future outcomes that ultimately change the lives of thousands of people as the future unfolds.

Whether we happen to choose a fast-moving queue or a slow-moving one in a fast-food restaurant, or stop to buy petrol in a service station now rather than at the next garage or the next day are examples of the many possible daily choices that generally go unnoticed but, like the preceding example, may lead to entirely different syncronicities. For this reason most scientists believe that it is impossible to predict future events in the lives of people with any certainty or to have a forewarning of natural disasters.[1]

However, many people have had intense feelings about the future, and some have seen visions, that enabled them to make accurate predictions or prophecies. How can this be, given that any of the thousands of choices we and others around us make daily have the potential to alter the course of our lives and the future?

University of Virginia psychiatrist Ian Stevenson has made several studies of reported premonitions of a number of natural disasters.[2] It seems that at times when a disaster is impending which will involve a large number of victims, several people do receive premonitions. One outstanding example involved the sinking of the *Titanic* on 15 April 1912.

On the *Titanic*'s maiden voyage across the icy waters of the North Atlantic the ship struck an iceberg in the dead of night and went down with the loss of 1513 lives. Stevenson collected reports of 19 individuals who had premonitions of the tragedy.[3] In some instances the sense of foreboding was so great that prospective passengers were actually persuaded to change their minds about sailing on the ship. Frank Adelman, a violinist, had booked a passage to New York for himself and his wife, but a few days before the departure from Southhampton in England, Mrs Adelman had a sudden premonition of danger and urged her husband to cancel the booking and travel on a later passage. He chose to resolve the matter by tossing a coin. Mrs Adelman won and they decided against sailing on the *Titanic*.[4]

Another equally persuasive wife who saved the life of her husband was a Mrs Shepherd of Nebraska who, after experiencing a vivid dream in which the *Titanic* sank, begged her husband by letter and telegram to take another ship. He followed his wife's urgings and cancelled his reservation in favour of another White Star Line steamship.

American theatre producer Henry B Harris was implored by a business associate William Klein not to sail on the *Titanic* after Harris cabled Klein about his booking. When Klein received the telegram he was filled with such a sense of impending doom that he promptly sent a return message with the warning. Harris replied that it was too late to change his plans and went ahead and boarded the ship with his wife. Only his wife was among the survivors. Another passenger, Richard Rouse, took his wife to see the ship he would be sailing on to America to set up their new home. When she saw the *Titanic* she was overcome with fear and tried to talk her husband out of going and to wait for a later passage. However, Mr Rouse reassured his wife that the ship was 'unsinkable' and went ahead with his plans. He was not among the survivors.[5]

Esther Hart was another woman who was gravely troubled by the 'unsinkable' label that had been bestowed upon the *Titanic*. She felt that such a claim was tantamount to defying God and that the ship would never make it to the other side of the Atlantic. Her pleading with her husband was unsuccessful and she reluctantly joined him with their seven-year-old daughter Eva for the voyage. Esther had a premonition that the ship would sink during the night and chose to sleep during the daytime and to remain awake at night. While Esther and her husband Benjamin were not among the survivors, little Eva Hart survived and, it seems, owed her life to her mother's night-time vigil.[6]

Mrs William Bucknell of Philadelphia was due to board the *Titanic* at Cherbourg in Normandy when she had an awful premonition that something terrible was going to happen to the liner. She confided her fears to her friend, Denver millionairess Mrs J J Brown, who persuaded her aboard. On the voyage Mrs Bucknell continued to have strong feelings that the ship was doomed, and shared her overwhelming concerns with other first-class passengers. Both Mrs Bucknell and Mrs Brown, who was to earn the title 'The Unsinkable Molly Brown' for her bravery and courage during the evacuation and later in the lifeboats, lived to tell the tale.

Several precognitive experiences where details of the disaster were seen ahead of time have also been reported. New York lawyer Isaac C Frauenthal had travelled to Europe for the wedding of his brother, Henry. The newlyweds, and Frauenthal, chose to return to America on the new liner *Titanic*. During the early part of the voyage Isaac revealed to his brother that just before boarding the ship he had had a vivid nightmare. In the dream he was on a big steamship that suddenly crashed into something and began to sink. He told Henry, 'I saw in the dream as vividly as I could with open eyes the gradual settling of the ship, and I heard the cries and shouts of frightened passengers'. Isaac became more alarmed when he had the same vivid dream a second time. When the ship hit the iceberg on the night of 14 April, Isaac at once insisted that the ship would sink and all three managed to escape drowning by finding places in a lifeboat.

Another clear precognitive vision was experienced by Mrs Blanche Marshall who watched with her family and servants as the *Titanic* steamed past the Isle of Wight shortly after leaving South-hampton. Suddenly she had a vision of the ship sinking and declared to those around her, 'That ship is going to sink before it reaches America. I can see hundreds of people struggling in the icy water'. Interestingly, Mrs Marshall also correctly predicted the sinking of the *Lusitania*, which resulted in almost as great a loss of life as on the *Titanic*. The Cunard liner was torpedoed by a German submarine off the coast of Ireland on 7 May 1915, and 1198 people lost their lives.

A very detailed precognition experience was told to Salvation Army captain W Rex Sowden in Kirkcudbright, Scotland, just three and half hours before the *Titanic* hit the iceberg. At 11 pm local Scottish time on the night of 14 April 1912, he sat at the bedside of a dying orphan girl named Jessie. Grasping his hand she suddenly exclaimed, 'Can't you see that big ship sinking in the water? Look at all those people who are drowning. Someone called Wally is playing the fiddle . . .!' With that the girl fell into a coma and died a short while later. Wallace (Wally) Hartley, an accom-plished violinist, was the bandmaster on the *Titanic*. He and his fellow musicians bravely stood their ground and played music and hymns to help calm the passengers right up until the *Titanic* slipped beneath the waves. All the band members perished.[7]

It seems that the mind of the dying girl somehow tuned into the future, and she was able to see and hear forthcoming events in quite some detail before they actually synchronised with space and time as we know it. This is yet another example which suggests that the closer the precognitive experience is to the event actually happening, the more detailed and comprehensive is the information about the future event.

Two unsuspected yet amazing precognitive experiences of the *Titanic* disaster were recorded as novels 20 years and 14 years before the event took place. In 1892, noted British journalist W T Stead wrote a nautical tale called *From the Old World to the New*. In the story a ship sinks after striking an iceberg in the North Atlantic Ocean. A number of survivors were picked up by the passing vessel *Majestic*, which was captained by an E J Smith.[8] The tale basically outlines the disaster but some of the information does not mirror the real-life event. For example, an E J Smith was the captain of the ill-fated *Titanic*, not the rescue vessel, and survivors were picked up by a vessel named *Carpathia*, not *Majestic*. Later in the chapter I will discuss how some researchers have noted precognition experiences which were very accurate in some details but contained incorrect information, somewhat like placing jigsaw pieces in the wrong puzzle. The alignment of E J Smith to the wrong vessel fits this scenario and may be an example of a poorly resolved image of a forthcoming event unwittingly experienced 20 years ahead of time. Furthermore, it is highly unlikely that the author realised he was being prophetic about his own death. Twenty years later Stead was one of the passengers who went down on the *Titanic*.

Some readers may see the details of Stead's novel as just one of those coincidences which happens occasionally. Given that hundreds of steamers crossed the North Atlantic where there were possibly thousands of icebergs, it seems quite reasonable that sooner or later a ship would hit an iceberg and sink. However, ships were not blindly crossing the ocean, such that a collision with an iceberg would be just a matter of calculated probability. Ships were navigated deliberately to avoid such objects and employed lookouts to prevent collision. Consequently, only a very small number of ships have actually hit an iceberg and sunk. It appears that the *Titanic* is the *only* ship to have hit an iceberg and sunk in the United States–European shipping lanes since Stead wrote his book.[9] As mathematician Jack Cohen, from Warwick University in England, points out in a recent *New Scientist* article on coincidences:

> . . . if something that seems spooky to you really does turn out to have a small sample space, that's when you should be really amazed.[10]

Given the incredibly small sample size of ships that sink in the North Atlantic as a result of hitting an iceberg, a particular novel, written by retired Merchant Navy officer Morgan Robertson six years after Stead's novel and 14 years before the *Titanic* sailed, is amazingly prophetic. Robertson's book was called *Futility*, and was published in 1898 by M F Mansfield in New York.[11]

The story revolved around the *Titan*, a huge, supposedly unsinkable passenger ship fitted with 19 watertight compartments and featuring watertight doors which closed automatically in the presence of water. Because the ship was deemed unsinkable, it carried only the minimum number of lifeboats required by law. These would hold only a quarter of the passengers and crew. The triple screw propeller British liner had a top speed of 25 knots. On her fourth voyage from New York to Southhampton, in April, with 2000 people on board, the *Titan* was attempting a record crossing when its starboard hull was severely pierced as a result of a collision with an iceberg in the North Atlantic, causing it to sink. Only two boat loads of survivors were rescued, the vast loss of life caused in part by a shortage of lifeboats.

This story is amazingly accurate in prophetic detail. Even the name *Titan* is very close to *Titanic*. The name was proposed in 1907 by Joseph Bruce Ismay, chairman of the White Star Line, when he announced plans for three vast, fast, luxurious transatlantic liners. The other two liners were to be called *Olympic* and *Gigantic*, with the *Olympic* to be built first.[12]

The *Titanic* was huge. At the time of its launch in 1911 it was the biggest ship in the world. Features on the ship included a double bottom, 16 watertight compartments each equipped with automatic watertight doors which could be closed from the bridge to make the ship 100 per cent watertight. As a further precaution, automatic float switches were provided under the floor near the watertight doors. Should any water enter any of the compartments, the doors would close automatically. It was also claimed that the ship could float with any two compartments flooded and since nobody could envisage anything worse, the *Titanic* was deemed 'unsinkable' in many of the articles written about her at the time. The *Titanic* was of a triple screw propeller design with a top speed of 24 to 25 knots. Her maiden voyage was in April, and from Southhampton to New York.[13] When she headed out into the North Atlantic, the *Titanic* was carrying a total of 2224 passengers.[14]

While in the North Atlantic, the *Titanic* collided with an iceberg which pierced its starboard hull in many places, causing five of the watertight compartments to flood. The watertight bulkheads did not reach high enough so that, as the bow of the ship sank, water spilled over the top of the bulkheads into adjoining compartments which also filled up.[15]

Although contemporaneous rumours that the *Titanic* was attempting a record crossing were allayed by the chairman of the White Star Line,[16] at the time of the collision the great liner was travelling at 22 knots, adjudged at the time to be too fast for the iceberg conditions. There was vast loss of life, 1513 persons in all, primarily because of a shortage of lifeboats. The *Titanic* carried only 1178 lifeboat places for the 2224 persons on board.[17]

Only 711 persons survived the tragedy, which is considerably more than the two lifeboats of survivors in Robertson's story. However, when one considers Robertson's choice of the name of the ship, that both ships sailed in the same month, both had triple screw propellers and a top speed of 24 to 25 knots, both were of similar size and displacement, both featured a similar number of watertight compartments with automatically closing watertight doors, both were carrying approximately the same number of people yet insufficient lifeboats, both were attempting a record crossing when they encountered an identical problem in the same stretch of water, Robertson's story becomes an amazingly accurate prediction of the disaster.

It seems that when Robertson was writing his story his mind received input signals similar to those received by the dying orphan girl in Scotland, years earlier. We have noted that fragments of these input signals that contained information about the future were received by a number of people in the form of feelings of impending tragedy, vivid dreams and waking visions. Some of those people who received the signals, such as Robertson and the dying girl, were not connected with the *Titanic*. Interestingly, another story about a great liner ramming an iceberg in the North Atlantic was rolling off the printing presses just as the *Titanic* was preparing to leave Southhampton. The May 1912 issue of *Popular* magazine contained a story by M C Garnette who is reported to have dreamed the details of the incident while on a recent voyage on board the *Titanic*'s sister ship the *Olympic*.[18]

Do these images that enter the mind come from an external mind that can see the future? Or is the future already present in some other dimension outside time and space as we know it and at times our minds unknowingly and accidentally cross a forbidden space into this other dimension? Or do we have here more evidence for destiny fields that control the history of this world and which in turn produce their own signals that can be received by the human mind? Is the true picture a combination of these scenarios?

In searching for clues to the answers to these questions it is useful to consider in more detail the background to the *Titanic* disaster. One revelation is the decision made to construct the so-called watertight bulkheads in the *Titanic* to only three metres above the waterline, compared to nearly 10 metres above the waterline in the earlier steamer the *Great Eastern*. The *Great Eastern* hit a submerged rock in 1862 which caused a gaping gash in the hull nearly three metres wide and 17 metres long, yet the steamer did not sink. Another component is that the lifeboat regulations at the time of the *Titanic* were hopelessly outdated. Under British regulations a ship of 46 000 tons such as the *Titanic* was not required by law to carry any more lifeboats than one of 10 000 tons, even though it would undoubtedly be carrying many more passengers and crew. These regulations meant that the *Titanic* only had to carry boats for 962 people when it could be carrying as many as 3547 passengers and crew. It is revealing that Alexander Carlisle, who led the team of naval architects designing the *Titanic*, is reported as having misgivings about the regulations and originally incorporated 64 lifeboats in the design. This number was later reduced to the mandatory 16 lifeboats, after discussions between the builders and the owners. This meant that with an additional four collapsible lifeboats there was a lifeboat seating capacity for only 1176 people.[19]

In 1912 there was an unusually large number of icebergs in the North Atlantic caused by a huge ice field that broke away from the ice mass during the mild winter and drifted south. During the week before the *Titanic* sailed, 20 ships reported seeing ice in the shipping lanes, and some ships had been forced to stop. The French Line's *Niagara* actually hit an iceberg and sustained minor damage. The *Titanic*'s course would take it right through the thickest part of the ice. On Sunday 14 April, the day of the disaster, the *Titanic* received six radio messages from nearby ships about ice ahead. These messages were effectively ignored by Captain E J Smith and his officers. The sixth message, received at 9.40 pm from SS *Mesaba*, reported a great number of large icebergs stretching for 50 kilometres across the path of the *Titanic*. It was reportedly never delivered to Captain Smith or the officers on watch. The speed of the *Titanic* was not reduced.

Sunday morning on White Star ships was supposed to include a boat drill where all passengers and crew would assemble in life jackets at their boat stations. Yet on this Sunday, Captain Smith omitted to call the drill.[20] That night an iceberg watch was ordered but the binoculars in the crow's nest had disappeared a couple of days before and had not been replaced. The lookouts on watch had only their natural eyesight to spot any icebergs ahead of the speeding ship. When the lookout did spot the iceberg it was less than 500 metres away. The ship hit the iceberg about 40 seconds later.[21]

Although distress rockets were fired and the night was clear and still, a nearby ship only 10 kilometres away and which could be seen by the crew of the *Titanic* ignored the distress signals and actually moved away. This ship has never been identified for certain. Some believe it was the cargo vessel *Californian*, while recent evidence suggests it may have been the Norwegian sealer *Samson* that was illegally sealing at the time. Officers on the *Californian* later told a court of inquiry that they did see flashes of white light in the sky and wondered if it was a sign of 'some sort of distress'. They chose to take no action, however.[22]

On that fateful night a number of other human decisions compounded the tragedy. The overall evidence clearly suggests that there was some sort of overwhelming destiny field which led a number of people to make the inappropriate decisions which sealed the fate of the *Titanic*. The watertight bulkheads were not high enough for a serious holing of the hull; there was no public address system to warn passengers of danger and emergency procedures; the number of lifeboats was inadequate; radio warnings of large icebergs were ignored; the decision was made to maintain top speed, and not to change course; the boat safety drill was omitted; the missing binoculars used by the crew in the crow's nest were not replaced; and distress rockets were ignored by the crews of at least one and possibly two ships nearby. If a strong destiny field surrounded this disaster in which a large number of lives were lost, then it is not unreasonable to expect that a large number of people might receive premonitions and for precognition signals to be received years earlier.

A considerable portion of this chapter has been devoted to the *Titanic* saga because much research into the tragedy has been carried out that provides high-quality collaborated evidence for the ability of humans to see the future ahead of it actually happening. The comprehensive detail of the studies of the sinking of the *Titanic* also provide a rich source of clues to the nature of the future.

Similar powerful premonitions and precognitive visions have been experienced in association with other major disasters, but these have not been as extensively documented. One example that appears to have involved a powerful destiny field occurred during the conquest of the mighty Aztec empire in Central America by the Spanish.

In the early 1500s the Aztec empire was experiencing its greatest glory. Montezuma II, the last Aztec emperor of Mexico, had enlarged the empire with successful military campaigns, and set up a gigantic political, military and religious bureaucracy. Like the *Titanic*, however, Montezuma's reign was also accompanied by forebodings of doom for the kingdom. These stemmed from a remarkable prophecy that was made in the year AD999 by the great Toltec King Ce Acath Topiltzin, who founded the city of Tula and led his people to civilisation. Physically, this king was described as having fair skin and a beard, which is intriguing given that the Aztecs were not fair-skinned and did not have beards. During a religious upheaval, the partisans of a war god drove Topiltzin in to exile. He sailed eastward and prophesied his return in the year of 'One Reed'.

This year occurred once in every Aztec time cycle of 52 years, with AD999 being a 'One Reed' year. Topiltzin predicted there would be signs in nature and omens to confirm the fulfilment of his prophecy was at hand.[23]

Signs and portents such as the ones he foretold were manifest in 1505, when there was a famine, and in 1507, when there was an eclipse followed by an earthquake. These natural phenomena were interpreted by Montezuma and his advisers as being the omens that heralded impending doom. It is reported that during a religious festival in 1508, Montezuma had a vision of a concourse of people advancing, massed as conquerors in battle array. They were riding what Montezuma thought were deer, no Aztec having seen a horse. That same year Montezuma's sister Paranazin experienced a trance in which she had a vision of an invasion. She saw great ships from a far country bringing to Mexico men in foreign dress who were armed, wore metal casques on their heads, and carried banners. These foreigners would become the masters of the Aztec lands.[24]

The tenth cycle of the 'One Reed' would fall in 1519. Montezuma and his astrologers believed that Topiltzin would return as the god Quetzalcoatl and destroy the kingdom.

From 1517, Spanish expeditions led by Hernandez de Cordoba and Hernando Cortez had been exploring the coasts along the Gulf of Mexico. In March 1519, Cortez landed on the coast of Mexico and discovered from the local Indians that Montezuma held him in awe. Cortez marched a small force of Spanish soldiers and 1000 Indian allies to Montezuma's capital Tenochtitlan (later rebuilt as Mexico City), and entered the city with virtually no resistance on 8 November 1519.

Montezuma believed the fair-skinned and bearded Cortez to be the fulfilment of the prophecy and received him with honour. Montezuma was later seized by Cortez in order to hold the country through its monarch. After an insurrection, during which Montezuma was killed, the mighty Aztec empire fell to Cortez on 13 August 1521.[25] The Spanish invasion had accurately fulfilled the reported visions of Montezuma and his sister and, in time, fulfilled a destiny predicted 520 years before.

One of the aspects of Topiltzin's prophecy involved signs in nature. Are earthquakes, famines, comets and eclipses also controlled by destiny fields? It is revealing that almost 1000 years before Topiltzin, Jesus Christ foretold that similar signs in nature would occur just before he returned to Earth with the angels of heaven. The signs would consist of unusual phenomena in the sun, moon and stars, such as the sun and moon darkening and stars falling in the sky. There would also be distress among the nations of the world, with famines and earthquakes in various places.[26] Jesus also foretold there would be similar signs just before the destruction of Jerusalem.[27]

The second coming of Jesus Christ has obviously not yet occurred for, according to the prophecy, when this event does happen the sky from the east to the west will be as bright as lightning,[28] every person on Earth will see the event happen[29] and believers will be gathered by angels to meet Jesus in the air.[30] Many people today believe that this prophecy will be fulfilled soon, and I will discuss the reasons for this in chapter 6.

Jesus' prophecy about the destruction of Jerusalem was fulfilled in accurate detail 33 years after his death. He predicted there would be many natural disasters beforehand but these would not be the main sign. Rather, when believers saw Jerusalem surrounded by armies, it would be a sign that the end was near and that they should flee to the mountains for refuge.[31] A siege wall would be built around Jerusalem and many in the city, including women and children, would fall by the sword, some would be taken captive and sent among the nations of the Roman Empire and Jerusalem would be destroyed to the point of being completely trodden down.[32] The magnificent Jewish temple in Jerusalem would be broken down to the extent that there would be not one stone upon another that had not been thrown down.[33] The plight of the people in the city would be so horrible that the like of such carnage would never have been seen up until then nor would ever be seen again.[34]

These prophecies would have seemed almost impossible to the Jews living in Jerusalem at that time. The city was held to be impregnable, being built with strong stone walls on a steep-sided mountain. When the siege did take place in AD66, it took four years for the city to be captured.

Within Jerusalem was the magnificent Jewish temple, that had been built by Herod the Great. This was built as an incredibly strong, fortified complex of stone galleries, balustrades and forecourts. Who could even imagine it being totally destroyed? In fact, when Titus, the commander of the Roman siege forces, did attempt to take the temple in the closing days of the siege in AD70, he found that rams and siege engines were powerless against its walls.[35]

Jesus' description of a carnage more terrible than anything ever experienced in the history of the world would have been almost incomprehensible to his listeners, yet as the eminent scholar and fellow of Trinity College at Cambridge University, Dr Frederick W Farrar, comments:

> Never was any prophecy more closely, more terribly, more over-whelmingly fulfilled than this of Christ ... Never was a narrative more full of horrors, frenzies, unspeakable degradations, and overwhelming miseries than is the history of the siege of Jerusalem.[36]

Farrar writes that:

> In that awful siege it is believed that there perished 1 100 000 men, besides the 97 000 who were carried captive, and most of whom perished subsequently in the arena or the mine.[37]

Such a massive loss of human life is likely to be associated with an extremely strong destiny field and, as the destruction of the Aztec empire by Cortez was predicted centuries beforehand, so too was the time of the destruction of Jerusalem and the end of the temple.

In the sixth century BC, the Hebrew wise man Daniel was an adviser to the great Babylonian king Nebuchadnezzar at the time when Babylon was the centre of science and astrology in the ancient world. Daniel prophesied the destruction of Jerusalem and the end of the temple.[38] The details of this amazing prophecy, which also predicted the advent of Jesus Christ and the date of his death in AD31 have been commented on by other scholars.[39] Jesus himself reminded his followers to take note of the particulars of Daniel's prophecy, and of the sign of the armies surrounding Jerusalem.[40]

Jesus' prophecies about Jerusalem, as unlikely as they seemed at the time, began to be fulfilled in a series of natural disasters which occurred between his death and the siege of Jerusalem. The Roman historian Tacitus (c. AD 56–120) reports that there were particularly severe hurricanes and storms in AD65, the year before the Jewish revolt. There were four major famines between AD41 and 54, including a very severe famine in Judea in AD44. Particularly bad earthquakes were also noted in this period—in Crete (AD46), Rome (AD51), Phrygia (AD60) and Campania (AD63). Tacitus also mentions the appearance of a comet at this time.[41] It is interesting that Jesus warned his followers that these signs were a matter of course and it was not until they saw Jerusalem surrounded by armies that they were to flee. This seems strange because how would one be expected to escape when the city was surrounded? We shall see, however, that again there seems to have been an overshadowing destiny field influencing the decisions of men.

In AD62, when Jerusalem was enjoying its greatest peace and prosperity, a melancholy maniac began traversing its streets warning its inhabitants of impending doom and crying out, 'Woe! Woe to Jerusalem. Woe to the city; woe to the people; woe to the Holy House.' He was later killed during the siege.[42]

Four years later in AD66 the Jews revolted and captured Jerusalem from their Roman rulers. Cestius Gallus, the Roman governor of Syria, led a recovery force of some 12 000 legionaries, 1000 cavalry and 15 000 auxiliary soldiers, concentrating his entire force upon Jerusalem. After surrounding the city, he gathered his troops for an assault and penetrated as far as the north wall of the temple. Then an astounding thing happened: Gallus withdrew his troops and placed himself strategically in such a poor position among the Judean hills that the Jews were able to attack his troops, killing more than 5000 infantry and nearly 500 cavalry.

It was at this time that the Christians in Jerusalem fled in accordance with the warnings of Jesus' prophecy 36 years earlier. This was the lull in the storm. Emperor Nero then appointed the highly successful Roman general Flavius Vespasianus to lead a further campaign against the Jews. Vespasianus set about capturing and massacring the inhabitants of the surrounding towns, with the plan to destroy Jewish centres outside Jerusalem and thus cut off supplies to the capital. This was achieved by the winter of AD67. War plans were affected by the suicide of Nero in AD68 and in AD69 Vespasianus was elected Emperor of Rome by his troops. He returned to Rome leaving his son Titus to capture Jerusalem. In the spring of the following year Titus appeared with an enormous army of 80 000 men outside Jerusalem.

The city was swarming with people, pilgrims having come from far and near to celebrate a religious ceremony called the Passover. A call to surrender was met with contempt and Titus began the final siege, assembling battering rams and siege engines against the wall. In order to stop Jews leaving the city and attacking his forces at night, Titus decided to seal off the city and ordered the erection of a 'circumvallatio'. With a huge effort the Romans constructed a massive, high wall of earthwork in a wide circle round Jerusalem, strengthened by 13 fortified strong points.[43] This unexpected action by Titus fulfilled in accurate detail the second part of Jesus' prophecy.

From this time starvation set in, and by July many areas of the city had fallen. Titus wanted to spare the famous sanctuary built by Herod the Great, but the refusal of the rebels to surrender and the impregnable nature of its walls forced him to set fire to the wooden temple gates to gain entry.

Then another amazing course of events took place. Still wishing to save the sanctuary, Titus ordered his soldiers to fight the fire that now began to spread. However, the beleaguered rebels seized the opportunity to make a violent attack. With remorseless slaughter the Roman legionaries drove the Jews back, but during the foray a blazing torch was flung through a high window into the most holy part of the temple. These rooms were panelled with old wood and flames quickly flared up. Titus saw the flames and personally took charge of the firefighting. He made every effort to get the soldiers to put out the fire. However, in what ran contrary to the famous tradition of Roman army discipline, the soldiers ignored the orders of their commander and spurred on by hatred and the hope of booty—for they had the impression the inner rooms of the temple were full of gold—they continued fighting. Thus the magnificent temple was burned down. When the rest of the city was captured, Titus ordered the whole city and the temple to be razed to the ground.[44]

The temple was thus totally destroyed as Jesus had prophesied. It was never rebuilt. All that remains to this day is part of the western wall of the temple courtyard, known as the 'Wailing Wall' or Western Wall, Jewry's most hallowed religious and historic site. The destruction of the temple despite the persistent and determined efforts of the great General Titus, who later became the Emperor of Rome, admits of an interpretation of the existence of a strong destiny field which had determined the future of Jerusalem.

Further evidence for a preordained destiny comes from the severity of the calamity, which was exacerbated not only by the stubbornness of the defenders who frustrated Titus' efforts to reduce the loss of life, but also by the fighting that took place among the defenders themselves. Rumours that the Jews swallowed their gold and jewellery to keep it safe led to the indescribable butchery of those caught fleeing the siege. In one night, 2000 people alone lost their lives in this way. Again, despite Titus' orders that this crime would be punishable by death, the practice continued in secret in the endless quest for plunder.[44]

A reluctant participant in the siege of Jerusalem, the historian Flavius Josephus, recorded the details of the promiscuous carnage that occurred, but I will not dwell on them.[45] Suffice to say that given the horrors of the starvation and butchery that took place, the death of more than one million people in this siege in AD 70 must rank it, as Jesus predicted, the most terrible tribulation in any city in the history of the world.

The Bible contains a large number of prophecies which accurately foretold future events. Old Testament scholar Professor J Barton Payne, who holds a doctorate from Princeton Theological Seminary, made a comprehensive study of prophecies and in 1973 published a 750-page *Encyclopaedia of Biblical Prophecy*.[46] Payne noted that there were 737 events predicted in the Bible with the majority being clearly fulfilled during biblical times. Others related to events in the future.

A group of American researchers from several universities, including Michigan State University, Ohio State University, Indiana University, North Texas State University and Sacramento State University, have studied the details of a number of biblical prophecies that were accurately fulfilled centuries after they were written. Their findings were published by Josh McDowell in his best-selling book *Evidence that Demands a Verdict*.[47] This meticulous research provides much valuable information about the nature of the future and, in particular, long-term precognition.

Some of the prophecies studied involved the predicted futures for several of the most powerful cities of the ancient world. It is fascinating that these prophecies referred to events that were to take place up to 1000 years or more later. This type of precognition or foreknowing would seem to require some sort of planned destiny for the future of the world, or that the history of the future as well as the past exists.

One of these amazing prophecies was written down by a young Hebrew priest by the name of Ezekiel around 586 or 587 BC, and concerned the future of the two powerful Phoenician cities of Tyre and Sidon. Ezekiel believed that he had received revelations of the future from the Creator God of the Hebrews. These revelations had been given as both warnings to the people and as a source of hope for the future.

Tyre and Sidon were the two most powerful Phoenician trading cities on the east coast of the Mediterranean Sea. Ezekiel predicted that many nations would come against Tyre.[48] First Tyre would be destroyed by the Babylonian king Nebuchadnezzar, who would construct siege walls against the city with a great army.[49] Then Ezekiel said that the walls of Tyre would be broken down and the debris scraped away to make her like a bare rock.[50] The stones and debris of the city would be thrown in the water and become a place for the spreading of nets.[51] The city would never be rebuilt.[52] The sister city Sidon, however, would not suffer the same fate. Instead Sidon would experience much violence and bloodshed but she would not be obliterated like Tyre.[53]

Ezekiel wrote his prophecy the year or so before Nebuchadnezzar II laid siege to the city in response to a revolt against Babylonian suzerainty. So his prediction about Nebuchadnezzar taking the city is perhaps not so remarkable given that the Babylonian king was successfully expanding his empire through military conquest. The events that followed, however, were a truly remarkable fulfilment of an amazing prophecy.

Tyre was the most powerful of all the Phoenician cities and was extremely well fortified. As a result, it held out for 13 years against the siege by Nebuchadnezzar's army. When the city finally fell in 573 BC, the Babylonian king found the city almost

empty. The majority of the people had moved by ship to a fortified island about a kilometre off the coast, taking their wealth
with them.[54] The island made terms of peace and recognised the
Babylonian rulership, and the island became the new Tyre. After
the destruction of the original Tyre, its sister city Sidon, which
was not attacked by Nebuchadnezzar, became the chief city of
Phoenicia. It is revealing that Ezekiel believed that Nebuchadnezzar was acting out a destiny decreed by God.[55]

The next part of Ezekiel's prediction came to pass 240 years
later, when Alexander the Great with his army was marching southward towards Egypt. Again the inhabitants of Tyre, feeling safe in
their fortified city, refused to cooperate. Alexander set about to lay
siege to the island. In an unexpected military strategy, Alexander
decided to build a stone causeway 60 metres wide and almost a kilometre long from the mainland to the island. For material for its
construction, his troops took the debris left from Nebuchadnezzar's
destruction of old Tyre and threw it into the sea. So much fill was
needed for the causeway that the site of old Tyre was scraped as bare
as a rock.[56]

Alexander took the city after a siege lasting seven months.
Today, fishermen from a small fishing village near the site continue
the tradition of spreading their nets on the stones of the causeway
that was once the great city of Tyre.[57] Ezekiel's predictions were
accurately fulfilled.

During the centuries following Alexander's conquest of Tyre,
the city never regained its former prominence. In Roman times
the city was famous for its manufacture of silk and for Tyrian
purple, a dye derived from murex snails. In 638 the city was
captured by Muslims. Later, in 1124, it was taken by the
Crusaders. In 1291, almost 1900 years after Ezekiel made his
prediction, the city was totally destroyed by the Muslims and has
never been rebuilt.[58] The present-day city of Tyre is not related

to the original city and is built down the coast from the original site.[59]

Sidon, on the other hand, exists today as the fourth-largest city of modern Lebanon, yet since Ezekiel's time it has been captured over and over again, first by the Persians in BC 351, then by Alexander the Great, the Seleucids of Syria, the Ptolemies of Egypt and the Romans. During the period of the Crusades, Sidon changed hands several times and more than once it was destroyed and rebuilt. It was destroyed again by the Mongols in 1260. Rebuilt by the Turks in the sixteenth century it was ravaged by an earthquake in 1837 and again rebuilt. Over a period spanning 1000 years, although its citizens were butchered and houses razed time after time, the city has always been rebuilt.[60] Its history accurately fulfilled Ezekiel's prediction of a bloody and violent future for the city yet without permanent destruction.

Space does not permit discussion of many of the other highly specific prophecies which accurately predicted the future history of a number of important cities of the ancient world, including Memphis, Nineveh and Babylon.[61] Taken together, these prophecies provide powerful evidence supporting the view that divine forces regulate the balance of political power of the nations according to a preordained divine destiny or 'plan'. It seems that the minds of men and women are influenced by the destiny fields created by this 'plan' so that their decisions ultimately lead to the fulfilment of this preordained future. By this same process the human mind can be 'told' of events that will happen hundreds and even thousands of years in the future.

Since the seers of biblical times there have been a number of people who seemed to have the ability to 'see' the future and make accurate predictions. The most famous is the French astrologer and physician Michel de Notredame (1503–66), known as Nostradamus. His fame rests on his book *Centuries* which was first published in 1555. The book contained 10 chapters of 100 quatrains which were four-verse prophecies. In the first two quatrains (I:1,2) he reveals that the source of his prophecies was a practice of divination, that was similar to crystal-ball gazing. Some students of his prophecies credit him with predicting various events in the history of the world and even into the next millennium.

For example, quatrains II:51 and II:53 appear to predict the great fire of London in 1666 and the plague which had preceded it the year before. Nostradamus wrote:

> The blood of the just will be demanded of London burnt by fire in three times twenty plus six. The ancient lady will fall from her high position and many of the same denomination will be killed.

The 'ancient lady' is interpreted as St Paul's Cathedral, which was destroyed in the fire and 'many of the same denomination' as those who fled from their homes to the stone churches for protection but subsequently died from the heat.[62] Quatrain II:53 reads:

> The great plague in the maritime city will not stop until death is avenged by the blood of a just man taken and condemned for no crime; the great lady is outraged by the pretence.

86

The 'just man' is interpreted as being King Charles I of England, who was beheaded in 1649 at the end of English civil war. The 'great lady' is interpreted as being the Church.[63] A particularly famous prophecy is quatrain V:33 which reads:

The city's leaders in revolt, will in the name of liberty slaughter its inhabitants without regard to age or sex. There will be screams and howls and piteous sights in Nantes.

This has been interpreted as a prophecy of the 'drownings' of Nantes under the Committee of Public Safety in 1793. The French Revolutionary terrorist Jean Baptiste Carrier was notorious for his atrocities against counter-revolutionaries at Nantes where he had large numbers of prisoners put on board vessels with trapdoors for bottoms, which were then sunk in the Loire.[64]

Another remarkable prophecy appears to refer to Hitler. Quatrain II:24 has been translated:

Beasts wild with hunger will cross the rivers, the greater part of the battlefield will be against Hitler. He will drag the leader in a cage of iron, when the child of Germany observes no law.

The original work used the name 'Hister' which the translator has changed to Hitler. It is revealing that interpreters before 1930 understood Hister to mean the river Danube, from its Latin name Ister. It is known that Hitler saw himself as portrayed in this and other quatrains by the mid-1930s and that Goebbels, the propaganda minister of the Third Reich, made great propaganda out of them in the prewar years.[65]

It can be seen from these examples that, at best, Nostradamus' prophecies are vague. French psychologist and statistician Michel Gauquellin points out that their mysterious obscurity, because of a 'kind of gibberish that was a mixture of many different languages', permits as many interpretations as once could wish.[66]

Nostradamus won lasting fame when on 10 July 1559, King Henry II of France died in a manner which seemed to be predicted in *Centuries*, published scarcely four years earlier. Quatrain I:35 reads:

> The young lion will overcome the old one on the field of battle in single combat: He will put out his eyes in a cage of gold; Two fleets one, then to die a cruel death.[67]

Some interpreters translate the fourth verse to read 'two wounds in one, then he dies a cruel death'.[68]

During the festivities celebrating the marriages of both his sister and his daughter, King Henry II of France took part in a jousting tournament. During a bout with Montgomery, the captain of the Scottish Guard, an accident occurred in which Montgomery's splintered lance pierced the king's helmet and entered his head just above the eye. Henry died 10 days later.

Gauquelin points out that there are some serious shortcomings to the view that Henry II's death fulfilled this prophecy. The standard interpretation has Montgomery as the young lion and Henry II as the old lion, because both used lions as emblems on their armour. However, Henry was only about six years older than his opponent and neither used a lion as an emblem on their coat of arms. Furthermore, the helmet of the king was neither gold nor gilded.[69]

Line three is even more dubious. The wound not only did not put out eyes or even one eye, but hardly touched the eye itself. A splinter lodged above the right eye. Line four is a complete failure. Some interpreters have tried to reconcile this with the events by reading *classe* as meaning 'wound' from the Greek *klasis* meaning a break or fracture, instead of translating *classe* as meaning 'fleet' from the Latin *classis*. It is rather inconsistent to use a Greek derivation here when, as Gauquelin points out, *classe* means fleet everywhere else in its many occurrences in Nostradamus' quatrains.[70] The prophecies of Nostradamus are therefore vague and controversial and do not provide particularly reliable data for our understanding of the nature of the future.

Another famous seer is the American woman Jeane Dixon, who in the early 1950s predicted President Kennedy's assassination. In 1952, as Dixon was entering St Matthew's Cathedral in Washington for morning meditations, she suddenly experienced a clear vision of the future. She saw before her in brilliant detail the White House. Almost immediately the numerals '1960' formed above it and, as she watched, a dark cloud spread over the numbers and the White House where a man was standing. The man was young, tall and blue-eyed with thick brown hair. An inner voice told her that he was a Democrat, elected to the presidency in 1960 and that he would meet a violent death while in office. Dixon's prediction that 'a blue-eyed Democrat President elected in 1960 will be assassinated' was later published in the 13 May 1956 edition of *Parade* magazine.[71]

In 1960, at 43 years of age, John Fitzgerald Kennedy, a Democrat from Massachusetts, was the youngest man ever to be elected President of the United States. Kennedy was assassinated while in office on 22 November 1963, and his funeral was held in the very church where Dixon had her vision of the event 11 years before.

It is reported that on that fateful morning both Jeane Dixon and John Kennedy had premonitions that he would be killed that day. Kennedy is reported to have told his wife that morning, 'If someone wants to shoot me from a window with a rifle, I can't stop him so let's not worry about him'.[72]

Jeane Dixon saw ahead of time the assassination of Mahatma Gandhi in 1948, the suicide of Marilyn Monroe and the death of the Secretary General of the United Nations Dag Hammarskjöld in a plane crash in 1961. In each case she saw a brief precognitive vision of the event about six months ahead of time. About four months ahead of time Dixon had repeated visions of the violent earthquake that rocked Alaska on 27 March 1964.[73] The accuracy of Jeane Dixon's predictions became quite well known, and on at least one occasion she was called to the White House to advise the President during a time of international political tension.[74]

Not all of Dixon's visions came to pass, however. For example, in the early 1960s Dixon had a vision of a holocaust occurring in the 1980s.[75] Did this event not occur because decisions were made that 'changed' the course of destiny, and averted another world war or did she see distorted signals of the future?

In another example, in 1962 Dixon saw that Sir Winston Churchill would die at the end of 1964.[76] Churchill had a stroke on 15 January 1965 and died nine days later—a prophetic miss of 24 days. Precognition experiences which are close but miss the mark may actually provide important clues to our understanding of how the future exists.

Jeane Dixon had the natural ability to spontaneously receive signals of future events. As we have seen, many people experience premonitions and some experience clear pictures of the future in dreams or, more rarely, in visions. These experiences, however, occur only perhaps once or maybe a few times in the lives of most people and generally are associated with the death of or an accident involving a close relative. Many people never experience a premonition of any kind. Jeane Dixon, on the other hand, seemed to tap into the premonition signals of people in no way related to her. Such ability is rare but nevertheless real, just like the people who can perform fantastic feats of mental arithmetic.

Shakuntala Devi, who lives in Bangalore in India, demonstrates her mental arithmetic ability in shows around the world. On one memorable occasion in Texas she correctly found the twenty-third root of a two hundred digit number in the incredible time of 50 seconds. Sometimes people who are mentally handicapped have this ability. They are known as 'autistic savants'. For instance, two American brothers can consistently outdo a computer in finding prime numbers even though they are both mentally retarded. A handicapped British man was able to correctly and almost instantly give the day of the week for any date, even from another century.[77]

Do these examples provide clues to our understanding of the future? Is the mechanism whereby we can know or see the future similar to the way some people can know the answer to very long mathematical calculations? This is in a sense knowing the future, given that it would take most mathematicians a much longer time to calculate the answer using written formulae.

We saw in chapter 1 how the Indian mathematician Ramanujan was shown his advanced mathematical formulae by a 'mentor' in his dreams. Joan of Arc had a similar experience when she was given directions by an 'angel' to lead her army to victory. She was one of the greatest heroines in history and her incredible precognitive experiences, documented in the official records of her trial for treason, provide further revealing clues about the puzzle of the future.

Joan of Arc was born in the French village of Dromremy in 1412. She was a hardworking, simple and exceptionally pious child. From the age of 13 she began to hear a 'voice' which was accompanied by a great light. As time went on she believed that the voice was that of the archangel Michael. Later, on occasions, she was able to see this angel and other 'angels' who also spoke to her. These 'voices' were to guide Joan throughout her life.

At that time, the crown of France was in dispute between the dauphin Charles, the son of the late King Charles VI of France and the English King Henry VI whose armies were occupying nearly all the northern part of the kingdom. The apparent hopelessness of the dauphin's cause by 1427 was exacerbated by the fact that, five years after his father's death, he had still not been consecrated at Rheims, the traditional place for the crowning of French kings, as Rheims was well within the territory held by the English. In 1428 the English had laid siege to the loyalist city of Orleans, surrounding it with forts. The voices told Joan that she would raise the siege of Orleans and lead Charles VII to his coronation at Rheims.

Following the directions of her voices, Joan had unparalleled success in leading the French army to a momentous victory at Orleans. Though only 17 years old, she marched the victorious soldiers to Rheims where Charles was crowned in great splendour. These achievements were a decisive factor in the revival of France during the crisis of the Hundred Years War.

Joan continued to lead the French armies but was unhorsed and captured in battle on 23 May 1430 by the Burgundians, who had allied themselves with the English. At the request of the University of Paris, Joan was handed over for judgement by Pierre Cauchon, the Bishop of Beauvais, in whose diocese she had been captured. Joan was tried not for her offences against the English king but because of her faith and morals. It was charged that Joan had claimed divine revelation, had prophesied the future and immodestly worn men's clothing.

The records of Joan's evidence under oath at her trial in 1431 are still preserved. It is clear from these documents that her voices were accompanied first by light and sometimes by figures who spoke clearly and could be seen clearly, just like ordinary people. The voices came mainly when she was awake and sometimes when she was aroused from sleep. One of the predictions she received from her voices was that there was a rusty sword with five crosses on it behind the altar in the Church of St Catherine of Fierbois. She sent for it and it was found and given to her.

The sword was in a coffer within the great altar of the church of Fierbois. None of the clerics nor the townspeople knew of its existence. After receiving Joan's request, a search was made in the coffer, which had not been opened for 20 years; that is, before Joan of Arc was born. The voices also warned her that she would be captured before Midsummer's Day. It is revealing that during her trial there was no serious attempt by her judges to invalidate her clairvoyance.[78]

The events of her trial are complex but Joan maintained her testimony concerning her voices to the end. The final outcome was that she was burnt alive at the stake. Almost 20 years later, in 1450, Charles VII ordered an inquiry into the trial, and two years later her sentence was revoked and annulled. On 24 June 1920, the French parliament decreed a national festival in her honour, held on the second Sunday in May. Yvonne M Lanhers, Keeper of the National Records Office in Paris, asserts that Joan exhibited the basic characteristics and stamp of a genuine prophet, following the tasks laid upon them by divine command.[79]

The records of the trial of Joan of Arc, who fought for the freedom of her people, provide strong evidence for the existence of an external mind which watches over the affairs of humankind. More evidence to support this view comes from a 'voices' experience told to me recently. Dr Merlene Spear is a local medical practitioner and the emergency medical officer for a large food manufacturing plant. One morning in 1984 she was driving to work at Wingham in northern New South Wales when she had an unforgettable experience. As Dr Spear approached a winding section of the road she heard a voice behind her ear say in clear musical tones 'Slow down'. Totally surprised and amazed she exclaimed out loud 'Pardon?' The beautiful voice repeated the audible command 'Slow down'. Totally overwhelmed by the experience she stopped her car just before a bend. Within seconds, a yellow sports car appeared, travelling at very high speed around the corner on her side of the road. Dr Spear estimated that the car was probably moving at a speed in excess of 150 kilometres per hour. If she had not obeyed the voice, she would have been very seriously injured if not killed.

In the previous three chapters I have reviewed the overwhelming evidence that many people have experienced premonitions, vision, voices or dreams that have been either precognitive, telepathic or clairvoyant. A precognitive experience is one that correctly shows unexpected future events. A telepathic event is one in which one person becomes aware of the thoughts of another mind. In a clairvoyant experience, a person obtains information about the location or physical properties of some distant object or event but not from someone else's mind. These types of experiences are referred to as paranormal or psi (psychic) experiences. Several prominent psychologists, such as Freud, Jung, W Stekel and M Boss, have strongly asserted the existence of paranormal experiences.[80] University researchers have found that between 15 and 67 per cent of people surveyed, including university students and people whose names appear in *Who's Who in America*, have had a paranormal experience.[81] Dr John Taylor, Professor of Mathematics at King's College in London, points out that in one extensive study, 1600 cases were documented of people who saw details of the past long before they were born. Do the past, present and future form a continuum of existence which at times the human mind can somehow connect with and see?

As I was writing this chapter, one of the secretaries at the research laboratories where I work told me of a powerful premonition she had experienced. While travelling home with her husband

and family after a long weekend holiday, about one hour away from home she experienced a very strong, overwhelming sensation that something terribly wrong had happening at home. When she arrived home she found that their house had been broken into and trashed. The contents of the refrigerator had been scattered over the kitchen floor and, judging by the smell, the break-in had occurred a day or two earlier, probably at the beginning of the long weekend. That incident had happened 12 years ago but was still vivid in her mind because it was so different from anything else she had experienced.

Given that paranormal experiences seem to be relatively common, we should be able to carry out scientific experiments in the laboratory to demonstrate these phenomena and perhaps in this way obtain more clues about the future. Such experiments already have been performed in several universities and we shall look at some of the amazing results in the next chapter.

Chapter Three

Scientific Experiments into Seeing the Future

On the evening of 18 February 1998, the popular radio station ABC Classic FM was broadcasting its usual program when listeners in the Inverell area of New South Wales noticed reception fade away. Local residents then began hearing mobile phone conversations on their radios. This freak effect lasted for about 10 hours before transmission returned to normal. Radio engineers did not know exactly how ordinary radios could have received the mobile phone signals.

A similar incident occurred in the southern New South Wales town of Cooma during September 1997. In various locations around the town, but not in all areas, residents who had their radios tuned to the local ABC station at a frequency of 1620 kilohertz found themselves receiving a commercial radio station broadcasting at 950 kilohertz. The rogue signal was sometimes soft and sometimes loud. In both incidents a signal, at a frequency which would normally not be received, was in some extraordinary way carried over to a frequency that could be received. In the Cooma incident, radio engineers thought that powerlines may be involved and, at one stage, the electricity to a large part of the town was turned off, but to no avail. It was not until after a severe electrical storm several weeks later that the problem rectified itself.

In both situations, radio receivers tuned for a particular signal received an entirely different signal from another part of the radio spectrum as a result of a freak set of conditions which occurred somehow by chance. These two incidents may provide some useful insights into our understanding of the future.

The majority of the precognitive-type episodes discussed in the previous chapters appear to have occurred randomly; that is, as if by chance. Somehow the human mind received signals about the future, signals it is not normally tuned to receive. For example, the average person may have about 100 000 dreams in a lifetime. One night they have a dream that is precognitive, like Mike Martin or Eryl Mai Jones. Was there a set of freak conditions in the brain at that time which enabled them to receive signals from the future?

The recipients of these dreams nearly always describe them as being unusually vivid and very different from ordinary dreams. Was reception facilitated because there was a strong destiny field involving a close partner or a tragic disaster? Are the signals from the future present all the time, like the mobile phone radiation, but our minds are not tuned to receive them? Do people such as Jeane Dixon have minds that are more easily tuned to receive signals from the future or from a mind outside time and space which can see both what lies ahead and what has happened in the past?

The wide variety of precognitive experiences in all different types of settings by people with vastly different backgrounds suggests that the signals from the future are present all the time, everywhere, just like mobile phone and radio transmission signals. The signals seem to be stronger the closer we are to the event actually happening, although, just as on rare occasions long distance radio signals can be received sporadically, good reception of future events can sometimes be received a long time beforehand. Events involving the lives of a large number of people or a turning point in the history of a nation seem to generate stronger destiny fields or signals of the future.

Our reception of these signals seems to depend on our state of consciousness. It is revealing that Corrie Ten Boom was meditating in prayer and listening to the first bombs falling when she had her vision of her family being taken away against their will. Those bombs meant that the enemy was coming. There would have been feelings of fear and uncertainty while at the same time her mind would have been especially open to receive thoughts. Similarly, Jeane Dixon had entered St Matthew's Cathedral for her morning meditations and was kneeling for prayer when she suddenly had her vision of the president. Her mind was in the act of worshipping God in the very place where the funeral service for the president would be held 11 years later. Dixon experienced some of her other visions spontaneously when listening to friends in conversation. It was as though a word or a sentence triggered a connection in her mind that facilitated her receiving the vision. While travelling on a plane to New York in November 1961, a friend of Dixon's confided to her about a woman who had threatened to commit suicide. As she said the word 'suicide', Dixon suddenly had a vision of a totally different person suiciding. The person in her vision was Marilyn Monroe and Dixon told her friend it would happen within the next year. On another occasion a different friend was discussing her trip abroad with Dixon. As the two women talked about plane travel, Dixon suddenly had the vision of the United Nations' Secretary General Dag Hammarskjöld's plane crashing.[1]

Precognitive dream experiences seem often to occur just as the recipient is waking. Such was the experience with Emperor Constantine's dream and on a number of occasions for Joan of Arc. These experiences suggest that given just the right conditions the human mind can, like radio receivers, receive signals it would otherwise ignore.

If signals from everything including the future are everywhere, we should be able to detect them anywhere. Furthermore, if the ordinary human mind is at times capable of receiving these signals, we should be able to do experiments and find the conditions under which we can tune our mind in to know of things happening elsewhere or in the future. It is revealing that Paracelsus, the sixteenth-century Swiss physician who pioneered the application of chemistry to medicine wrote:

> Man also possesses a power by which he may see his friends and the circumstances by which they are surrounded, although such persons may be a thousand miles away from him at that time.[2]

So what do modern science and recent experiments in the areas of telepathy, clairvoyance and precognition reveal about these things?

One of the problems scientists encounter in this type of research is the difficulty of differentiating between true clairvoyance or precognition and mere guesses or chance results. For example, before we toss a coin we ask a test subject to predict which side it will land. They make their prediction and the coin lands as forecast. Was the result a genuine prediction or was it correct by chance? In this case there is a one in two chance or 50 per cent probability of guessing the correct answer. If, however, we repeat this experiment 10 times and our subject accurately predicts which way the coin will land each time, even though sometimes it lands heads and other times tails, the result is less likely to have occurred by chance. The calculated probability of this happening as a result of 10 correct guesses is about one in 1000. The more experiments that can be done where the probability of the result occurring by chance is very low, the more evidence we have for a genuine telepathic or precognitive experience.

One of the simplest experiments that has provided very strong evidence for the existence of a telepathic effect involves the ability of many people to tell when someone is staring at them from behind. Dr Rupert Sheldrake from Cambridge University has carried out thousands of experiments where blindfolded subjects sitting with their back to a glass window have to indicate when a person is staring at them through the glass. His results give powerful statistical evidence for the existence of the 'sixth sense'.

Just as with any other human ability, some people turn out to be much better at staring or being stared at than others. Some individuals have a success rate approaching 90 per cent. From a statistical point of view, however, the 'high performers' could skew the results. So Sheldrake has reanalysed his data using a statistical technique which removes the impact of high performers. The exact score is ignored and instead, the number of times people have scored above, equal to, or below 50 per cent is counted. To the surprise of the critics, the results are the same. Sheldrake reports: 'Everyone who has seen the data agrees there is an effect'.[3]

So what is this mysterious effect and how does it work? Sheldrake believes that the act of looking generates a field which the subject can detect, that the observer and the observed are somehow linked. This is an important hypothesis which we shall examine in more detail in the next chapter.

Recently I tried an experiment at home. My teenage daughter was on the phone, engrossed in conversation, with her back to a glass sliding door. I stood about 2 metres from the door and stared at the back of her head. About 10 seconds later she turned right around and looked at me with a questioning expression on her face.

In another example, a friend of mine was servicing a water pump about 15 metres down a narrow, gently sloping disused mine tunnel. Suddenly he had an intense feeling that he was not alone. He turned around and behind him he saw the head of a large venomous brown snake peering over the edge of the entrance to the tunnel. My friend described how the feeling was so intense that it distracted him while he was concentrating on the job of reassembling the pump. Anecdotal though they may be, these observations add further support to Sheldrake's hypothesis of the existence of some other type of communicating 'field'.

Extensive scientific studies of the phenomenon of telepathy and clairvoyance were pioneered by Dr J B Rhine and his colleagues at Duke University in Durham, North Carolina. They performed large numbers of tests during the 1930s and '40s with some remarkably significant outcomes. The results are reported in their important book *Extra-Sensory Perception After Sixty Years*.[4] Rhine and his co-workers found that it was possible to obtain results that are statistically significant when subjects are tested for telepathy, clairvoyance and even precognition.

For example, in one experiment, the investigator and the subject were in different buildings 100 metres apart. The researchers used a special pack of 25 cards divided into five equal sets with one each of five different pictures: a circle, a square, a cross, three wavy lines and a star. The investigator would shuffle the pack and place it face down. The subject would then try to visualise the order of the cards in the pack. At agreed times the investigator separated cards from the pack and the subject recorded his or her impressions of what the cards were. At the end of the pack the order of the cards was recorded and sealed in an envelope. The subject also sealed his or her answers in an envelope and both were sent to Dr Rhine for analysis. The total number of guesses was 1850, of which one-fifth or 370 would be expected to be correct by pure chance. However, the actual number of successes was far above that at 558. The probability of this occurring by chance was less than one in one hundred million.[5]

Tests of a similarly high level of success were obtained with 66 subjects who were selected at random, that is, not because they possessed some psychic ability, and involved a total of 96 700 guesses. In this particular set of experiments, the probability of the results occurring by chance was calculated to be less than one in one hundred thousand million.[6]

In the 1930s and '40s, D Martin and F Stribic at the University of Colorado also obtained high levels of success. The test involved 10 packs of the special cards described earlier, but the subject was asked to visualise the order of the cards in only one of them. After repeating the experiment 11 times, it was found that one subject had scored an average of 8.17 correct cards per pack. Yet if his guesses were applied to the other nine packs, which he had not attempted to visualise, his average score was only 5.02 per pack, which is very close to the pure chance value of 5. This type of experiment provides powerful evidence for clairvoyance.[7]

Since the pioneering work of Rhine, more fascinating and involved experiments have been carried out. One such piece of research was reported by R Targ and H Puthoff at the Stanford Research Institute in the highly respected science journal *Nature*, in 1974. A subject with well-known paranormal abilities was chosen. For one set of experiments he was locked in a double-walled steel room which provided visual, acoustic and electrical shielding. For another set of experiments the subject was located in a special double-walled and copper-screened Faraday cage in the Engineering Building at Stanford University. This cage provided additional shielding against radio waves.

In the first set of experiments the subject was asked to reproduce line drawings which were to be drawn outside the room after he was isolated. The objects for the line drawings were chosen in a variety of ways, such as opening a dictionary at random and choosing the first word that could be drawn, or drawings prepared by independent scientists or computer generated images.

The subject produced drawings for 10 objects. The objects and the drawings were published in *Nature* and some are amazingly accurate. For example, a bunch of grapes was drawn for a bunch of grapes, a bird flying for a seagull flying, a horse for a camel. Other responses were much less accurate, but each drawing contained some characteristics of the original target. In fact, two independent judges matched each of the response drawings to the target drawings with no error. For either judge the probability of this occurring by guesswork is one in 30 million. The Stanford researchers concluded that, 'In certain situations significant information transmission can take place under shielded condition'.[8]

In another experiment the researchers took subjects with no previously known paranormal abilities and tested their ability to visualise what another person was doing some kilometres away. One of the most successful subjects was former California Police Commissioner Pat Price. Locations about 30 minutes' drive away were chosen by a double blind protocol. Two to four experimenters would drive to the remote location and remain there viewing the location for 30 minutes. During that time the subject, who had remained behind closeted with another experimenter, sometimes in a Faraday cage, would tape record his or her impressions of what the other experimenters were doing. Since the experimenter remaining with the subject at the university was in ignorance about both the remote location and the pool of location choices, he was free to question the subject to clarify his description.

In the case of Price it was found that he was able to describe correctly remote locations such as buildings, docks, roads and gardens that were being viewed by the other experimenters. Locations chosen included the Hoover Tower, a radio telescope, a nature reserve, a marina, a drive-in theatre, a church, plazas and a park. Sometimes the description contained highly accurate details of the type of structural materials, colour and the activities going on at the site. However, the descriptions also contained inaccuracies as well as correct statements, as though the information channel was imperfect and carrying noise as well as the correct signal, or as if the image was not clearly resolved. In a typical example, Price correctly described a park-like area containing two pools of water, though he thought they were used for water filtration rather than their correct use as swimming pools. He also included in his drawing some tanks which were not present at the target site.[9]

To obtain an evaluation of the accuracy of the remote viewing or telepathy, the results were subjected to independent viewing on a blind basis by five Stanford Research Institute scientists who were not otherwise associated with the research. The judges were asked to match the nine locations, which they independently visited, against the typed transcripts of the tape-recorded descriptions of the subject.

The transcripts were unlabelled and presented in random order. The judges were asked to find a narrative which they would consider the best match for each of the places they visited. Of the 45 selections (five judges and nine choices), 24 were correct. The probability of this assignment occurring by chance was calculated as being one in 80 billion. The researchers concluded that somehow information about a remote location could be received by humans. They suggested that this perceptual ability may be widely distributed in the general population, but because the perception is generally below an individual's level of awareness, it is repressed or not noticed.[10]

The Stanford Research Institute experiments were carried out by researchers at a number of other universities with the results indicating successful remote viewing or telepathy. These findings were reported at several symposia held by the Institute of Electrical and Electronics Engineers in the United States during 1976 and 1977.[11] Details of subsequent remote viewing experiments at Stanford, including photographs of the target locations and objects, together with the amazing responses from subjects who drew the impressions that came to their minds, were published by the American Association for the Advancement of Science in their *Selected Symposia* series.[12]

The use of steel rooms and Faraday cages means that the telepathy phenomena are unlikely to involve electromagnetic thought waves or any form of electromagnetic radio-type waves. This puts telepathy outside the realm of current scientific knowledge and these findings have attracted much criticism from sceptics' organisations.[13] However, while these experiments are sometimes dismissed as sloppy pseudo-science, there has recently been more use of rigorous experimental methods in this area of research. A study of over 1000 research papers covering the areas of parapsychology, psychology and animal behaviour, medical sciences, other biological sciences, physics and chemistry revealed that in parapsychology research, blind methods were used in more than 90 per cent of the papers. In the other areas of research, blind methods where the subject or the analyst does not know exactly what is going on were used in less than 10 per cent of the reported experiments.[14]

Since the 1980s, very rigorous experiments demonstrating telepathy, or 'communication anomalies' as some scientists prefer to call it, have been performed at the Psychophysical Research Laboratories in New Jersey by Dr Charles Honorton. In the experiments the subjects being tested for telepathy were isolated in a steel-lined cubicle with walls 30 centimetres thick. Two halves of a ping-pong ball were taped over the subject's eyes and headphones playing white noise (random sound) covered the ears. Three metres away in a second padded and shielded cubicle, a 'sender' was concentrating on a television film of an object and trying to transmit the image telepathically.

In a typical experiment, the sender was repeatedly shown a video clip randomly chosen from 160 stored clips. The subject or receiver was shown four clips, one plus three decoys. The receiver scored a direct hit if the target scoring the highest rating was the same target that had been viewed by the sender. The likelihood of scoring a hit was 25 per cent. After 354 trials, the overall hitting rate was found to be 34.5 per cent. This result provided strong statistical evidence under first-class experimental conditions, that the phenomena of telepathy is real.[15]

Honorton used over 240 subjects not noted for any telepathic ability, yet some of the results are very exciting. For example, one sender was concentrating on a television film of an eagle. In the receiver's chamber the blindfolded subject listening to white noise began to describe:

> I see a dark shape of a black bird with a very pointed beak with his wings down ... Almost needle-like beak ... Something that would fly or is flying ... like a parrot with long feathers on a perch. Lots of feathers, tail feathers, long, long, long ... Flying a big huge, huge eagle. The wings of an eagle spread out.[16]

Results such as these have led Susan Blackmore, a psychologist at the University of Western England in Bristol and a noted debunker of psychic claims, to comment:

> I have come to the conclusion that Honorton has done what the sceptics asked, that he has produced results that cannot be due to any obvious experimental flaw ... He has pushed the sceptics like myself into the position of having to say it is either some extraordinary flaw which nobody has thought of, or it is some kind of fraud—or that it is genuine ESP.[17]

Research has also been carried out which provides evidence for precognition. In these experiments subjects have seen events happen in their minds ahead of time; in other words, they have seen the future under conditions carefully controlled and scrutinised by researchers.

In 1977 John P Bisaha, Assistant Professor of Psychology at Mundelein College in Chicago, and Brenda J Dunne, a doctoral student at the University of Chicago, presented a paper to the Institute of Electrical and Electronics Engineers which was similar to the Price remote viewing experiments at the Stanford Research Institute. In this paper, however, the research described statistical evidence for precognition; that is, remote viewing of the future.[18]

One of the 1977 experiments by Bisaha and Dunne was filmed by a television crew from CBS *News Magazine*. Part of the television crew remained with the 'percipient', or subject, at Mundalein College in Chicago. At exactly 1 pm the percipient was asked by the CBS interviewer what they visualised the agent would be doing at 2.15 pm. After a pause the person went on to describe—in front of the television cameras—a church with pews, triangular turrets, heavy wooden doors and a row of long thin windows. Meanwhile, the other part of the television crew had driven to downtown Chicago where at a scheduled time one of the group activated a random number program on a hand calculator to select one of ten envelopes prepared earlier by other members of the CBS television staff. Each envelope contained directions to a different target location accessible by a 30-minute drive. The target thus randomly selected was the Rockefeller Chapel on the campus of the University of Chicago. On arrival at the chapel just before 2.15 pm, the agent concentrated his thoughts on the scene and the crew videotaped his behaviour as well as scenes of the chapel target. The videotape of this amazingly accurate example of precognition was featured in an episode of CBS *News Magazine* broadcast nationally in the United States in January 1978.[19]

Brenda Dunne decided to pursue these early experiments further and obtained the support of Robert G Jahn, Professor of Aerospace Sciences and Dean Emeritus of the School of Engineering and Applied Science at Princeton University. Initially Jahn was sceptical and far from convinced of the validity of the purported phenomena. To assess the possibilities indicated by earlier experiments more systematically he undertook to organise, fund and supervise a substantial research program. This program was formally established in 1979 under the title Princeton Engineering Anomalies Research (PEAR). Over the next decade this group amassed a formidable amount of data supporting mind–machine interactions and precognition. The results involved the acquisition of information about geographic locations remote in distance and time and inaccessible by any known sensory communication channel.

The subjects involved in the experiments were men and women of various ages and backgrounds. None of them had any claimed extraordinary or 'psychic' abilities. Each one was required to generate a written description of an unknown geographical target where the agent would be stationed at a prescribed time. The agent would typically spend 10 to 15 minutes at the target, beginning at the assigned time and writing down his or her impressions of it. As in the example described earlier, the target visited by the agent was selected randomly and after the isolated percipient had recorded his precognitive vision. In some experiments the target was chosen spontaneously by the agent when in some remote location unknown to the percipient.

By late 1987, 334 formal trials involving 40 percipients had been carried out. The results ranged in accuracy from virtually photographic precision through to total irrelevance. The overall results, however, provided consistent evidence that under certain conditions we can not only see the future with significant resolution, but also, in some instances, the past. Let me describe some examples.

An agent visited a railway station 8 kilometres away. Thirty-five minutes beforehand the percipient saw in his mind a train station with its posters, advertisements and benches.[20]

An agent visited the Radio Telescope at Kitt Peak, in Arizona,

3500 kilometres distant from the percipient. Forty-five minutes beforehand the percipient described:

> ... rather strange yet persistent image of [agent] inside a large bowl—a hemispheric indentation in the ground of some smooth man-made material like concrete or cement. No colour. Possibly covered with a glass dome. Unusual sense of inside/outside simultaneity. That's all. It's a large bowl. (If it was full of soup [the agent] would be the size of a large dumpling!)[21]

An agent visited a terrace home with a balcony in Milan, in Italy, 6500 kilometres away. There were quite a number of shrubs and small trees on the balcony, which was on the fifth floor. Five and a half days earlier the percipient visualised:

> ... agent sitting on a small porch or balcony surrounded by a stone or brick wall, may be waist high ... A few trees, not necessarily on street—maybe on balcony—flowers in pots ...[22]

An agent visited a large suspension bridge over the River Danube, in Bratislava, Czechoslovakia, 9000 kilometres away. At one end of the bridge there are two characteristic pylons with a saucer-like disc on top and a ferry is passing underneath. Nearly 24 hours beforehand the percipient described:

> I have the feeling that [the agent] is somewhere near water. I seem to have the sensation of a very large expanse of water. There might be boats. Several vertical lines, sort of like poles. They're narrow, not heavy. Maybe lampposts or flagpoles. Some kind of circular shape. Almost like a merry-go-round or a gazebo. A large round thing. It's round on its side, like a disc, it's like a round thing flat on the ground, but it seems to have

height as well. Maybe with poles. Could possibly come to a point on top. Seeing vertical lines again. Seems to be a strong impression, these vertical lines. No idea what they can be . . . A definite sensation of being outside rather than in. Water again . . .[23]

Visions of the past were also experienced by some subjects. For example, an agent had visited the ruins of Urquhart Castle on the banks of Loch Ness, in Scotland, 5600 kilometres away. Fourteen and a half hours later the percipient was asked to describe any impressions about where the agent had been. The following retro-cognitive description was written down:

rocks; uneven holes; also smoothness
height
ocean-dark, dark blue
whitecaps
waves; booming against rocks?
on mountain or high rocks overlooking water
dark green in distance
gulls flying?
pelican on a post
sand
a lighthouse?—tall structure-round with conical roof
high windows or window space with path leading up to it
or larger structure similar to a castle
[Here there is a sketch of a castle abutment on the transcript] . . .[24]

The Princeton researchers developed an elaborate protocol for conservatively estimating the probability of precognitive descriptions being accurate by chance. When all the data from the 334 trials was analysed, the probability that the PEAR results were a result of chance or guesswork was calculated to be less than two in one hundred billion.

Jahn and Dunne go on to make the observation that the overall remote perception case which involves both precognition and retro-cognition, does not rest predominantly on a few outstandingly accurate perceptions immersed in a sea of chance results. Instead, the most convincing evidence rests on the consistent margin above that expected by chance which steadily accumulated over a large number of trials. For example, about 14 per cent of the 334 trials are individually significant by the 'less than 5 per cent probability by chance' criteria. However, over 62 per cent of the trials score above the chance mean.[25] These results provide first-class experimental evidence that the phenomenon of precognition is real.

Jahn and Dunne are also quick to point out the need to guard against excessive reaction to, or dependence on, extraordinary incidental results. For this reason they were careful to work only with very large quantitative databases acquired under systematic and rigorous protocols. Notwithstanding this caution, some of their anecdotal results that were not included in the data analysed may reveal useful information on the nature of the future.

For example, in one exploratory trial a percipient in Princeton provided a reasonably accurate precognitive description of a street scene in Paris where the agent was immersed in the typical hustle and bustle of traffic flow and shopfront paraphernalia. The subject also perceived an image of a medieval knight in full armour somehow involved in this pattern, and acknowledged this unlikely element in his free-response transcript. The agent had no corresponding feature in his target description but, after reading the perception, recalled that he had been standing in front of a government building ornamented with statuary of historical military figures attired in period dress. One of these closely matched the percipient's description.[26]

In another instance, an agent selected as a target the components of the Saturn moon rocket at the NASA Space Center at Houston, in Texas. The percipient in Princeton described an indoor scene with the agent playing on the floor with a group of puppies—a complete 'miss', both impressionistically and analytically. Later that evening, before learning any details of the perception, the agent visited a friend's home where he played at length with a litter of newborn pups, one of which he decided to purchase.[27]

In a somewhat similar case, an agent en route to the target of a gambling casino in Nevada stopped at a service station and amused himself for a while by attempting to ride a collapsible bicycle. The perception transcript, dictated in Chicago, included nothing relevant to a casino but featured an accurate description of the agent's clumsy attempt to ride the bike.[28]

A slightly different precognitive scenario was recorded when an agent, who had chosen an indoor seminar room in a Montana lodge as the target, let his mind wander to a scene just outside the building. He focused on a low stone wall, tree, and a picnic table, all of which were then noted in the target description. The percipient in New Jersey recorded nothing about the interior scene but was virtually photographic in their identification of the details and ambience of this external area.[29]

In each of the above examples the percipient's description yielded correct information, not about the target, but about an adjacent event or location. This being so, we might expect that the human mind could possibly see impressions of a number of adjacent events—even well into the future or into the past.

Both the Stanford and Princeton research suggest that signals from the past, present and future are ubiquitous. But how is our reception of these signals activated? How can we tune our mind to receive the future or the past?

At the dinner for the Parapsychology Convention held in Utrecht in 1976, Sir John Eccles, the 1963 Nobel Laureate in Physiology, said in his speech:

> The most paranormal thing in all is how I can move my finger when I so will it. The mind is the problem to explain in any parapsychological investigation.[30]

In the light of the above research, perhaps the most paranormal thing of all must now be how the mind can will to see the past, present and future, or receive signals from minds in a different space-time reality. In the beginning of this chapter I noted that radios only received signals in the frequency range they are set for. Of course, radios have the capacity to receive signals at vastly different frequencies. This function is a matter of tuning.

The evidence I have reviewed so far suggests that we can tune our minds to receive signals from other minds, but that it is not easily achieved in our western culture. On the other hand, as I have already discussed, many primitive peoples seem to have telepathic ability; that is, the ability to tune the mind to receive signals from other minds.[31] During dreams, and at other spontaneous moments, the western mind seems to inadvertently tune into these signals, but generally speaking we seem to be unaware of this ability.

There is one area of human precognition research that remains to be discussed and that is the epidemiological evidence. In the early 1950s a study was made of 28 serious railroad accidents in the United States in which 10 or more people were injured. The counts of the numbers of passengers aboard the trains on the days of the accidents were noted as were the counts on the seven days preceding the accidents and on the days two, three and four weeks before the accidents. It was found that the number of passengers was significantly smaller on the days of the accidents compared with preceding days. This data can be interpreted as indicating that many passengers had a subliminal precognitive impression of the impending accident and without being aware of why they did so, they changed their plans so that they did not travel on that train.[32]

The experiments reviewed in this chapter provide convincing evidence that the human mind can see the future. But many questions remain. Does the past, present and future exist in some dimension outside time and space as we know it? Does the human mind make contact with another mind or minds operating in a different dimension of reality, and who somehow know the future and the past? Or is there some other explanation for the evidence I have presented? In the next chapter we will look at the fascinating evidence for a scientific model that explains the future and the past.

Chapter Four

Destiny Fields: Towards a Scientific Understanding of the Past, Present and Future

On an August morning in northern Michigan in the United States, a monarch butterfly crawls out of its cocoon. As nutrients are pumped through its veins, its wings quickly expand and harden to reveal the beautiful orange and black patterns that identify this species. At first glance this newly emerged butterfly seems unlikely evidence for the existence of destiny fields but as we shall presently see, the behaviour of this insect born in the autumn will be radically different from that of its parents and possibly grandparents born in the spring and summer.

The monarch is one of the most familiar of the North American butterflies, being prolific during spring and summer throughout Canada and the United States. The species is probably best known for its unusual relationship with the milkweed for, despite the fact that the plant's leaves are poisonous, this is the only place that female monarchs will lay their eggs. After hatching, a monarch caterpillar grows rapidly while devouring the milkweed leaves. In the process, large amounts of the plant's toxic chemicals are absorbed. Fortunately the caterpillar is protected by an immunity that will be passed on with the poison to the butterfly. Weeks later, when the monarch flashes its striking orange and black wings, the entire bird community receives and usually heeds its unmistakable message: 'I taste terrible, leave me alone.'

During the summer, up to several generations of butterflies mate, lay eggs and die. But with the arrival of autumn the monarch's liaison with the milkweed draws to an end as the plants go to seed for the winter. At this time, newly hatching butterflies undergo a significant transformation of their own. Sexual behaviour and egg production cease as a series of hormonal changes equip it for a life span that will last for almost eight months. This is almost six times longer than its parents and even grandparents that were born during the spring and summer. This longevity is absolutely vital for the monarchs have only one way of surviving the freezing temperatures of the north—a migration to a warmer climate.

Of all the migrations undertaken in nature, the monarch's flight to its over-wintering grounds is one of the most astounding. It is a journey with two primary destinations. The monarch population living west of the Rocky Mountains moves towards the coast of California, and those east of the Rockies head towards Mexico. Some monarchs fly from Nova Scotia, in Canada, to the mountains of Mexico, some 5000 kilometres away. This journey often includes a flight of more than 600 kilometres over the waters of the Gulf of Mexico. Exactly where these butterflies spend their winter remained a mystery until January 1975, when Dr Frederick Urquhart who had devoted much of his life to searching for their place of hibernation, discovered millions of monarch butterflies hanging in the trees of remote forests in rugged volcanic mountain ranges approximately 200 kilometres west of Mexico City. Since 1975, about 30 different wintering colonies have been identified in this region. It seems that this secluded forest meets all the critical climate and food demands necessary to sustain the estimated 100 million monarchs that hibernate there each year. The butterflies remain there until the arrival of spring, when they once again fly north to the new crop of milkweed to lay their eggs which will become the new generations of short-lived monarchs.[1]

One of the questions that puzzles scientists is how does this tiny insect, about 4 centimetres long, navigate unerringly to a place it has never seen or been to before? Monarchs can be taken hundreds of kilometres off course and still find the way to their destination.

Recently it was discovered that the butterflies appear to have a built-in compass that enables them to navigate using the position of the sun.[2] It appears that the monarch can detect polarised light, which means it can determine the angle of the sun even on cloudy days.

Navigation by the sun requires at least two sightings of the sun's position relative to the horizon to be taken at two different times. The first measurement can be used to draw a line on a map if one has an accurate chronometer and an almanac that gives the sun's position relative to Greenwich time. The second measurement gives another line, and the point of intersection of the two lines is the approximate position on the map. If the monarch used a similar system it would have to have a built-in almanac of the sun's position relative to date and time, an accurate internal clock and a navigational computer to solve the equations.

Jules H Poirier, a senior electronics engineer who was responsible for designing navigational components for the Apollo moon rockets and other US space projects, is fascinated by the navigational achievements of the monarch. He points out that designing navigation equipment to take humans beyond the confines of this planet and safely back again took an enormous amount of intelligent effort. The fact that the monarch can do its unbelievable feats with such an amazingly miniaturised 'control centre' would require a level of design engineering which demands an overwhelmingly great intelligence.[3] Even if the butterflies were equipped with such an intelligent navigation system we still have not answered the question 'How do they know where to go?'

Imagine for a moment that we grew up as orphans from birth. If we were given a sextant, an almanac, a chronometer, a map and a set of instructions on how to do navigational calculations and were told to go to the place where our grandparents spent the winter, our first question would be, 'What is the location of this place?' All the navigation aids and maps are useless unless we somehow know 'where' to go.

But one day we may get a powerful feeling that we have to go to a certain place. It may be like the feelings experienced by the mothers who, as described in the introduction, 'knew' that something terrible had happened to their children; or the people who had premonitions that the *Titanic* would sink. If we follow the intuition of this powerful feeling and, lo, we do come to the place where our grandparents spent winter—thereby fulfilling our destiny and finding all our cousins are there too—then we would have convincing evidence for the existence of an external mind controlling our destiny.

The thought from this mind would be like a gravitational or magnetic field—drawing a response from our consciousness whereby our decisions cause us to align ourselves with the intentions of the external mind. Along the way we may have made detours to find food, or corrections for being blown off course by storms. Our journey would have been different in detail from that of our cousins, who would have followed a slightly different path and encountered different obstacles. We would be exercising free will, making choices, but always within limits. Although we could choose to do so, we did not go off in a different direction because of the overwhelming desire to follow our intuition. The destiny field, like the force of gravity, ensured that we fulfilled a preordained future by spending winter as our grandparents did.

The problem that the monarch butterfly has—that is, to know where to go to survive the winter—is in many ways similar to our dilemma regarding knowledge of the future. Is it possible that the mystery of animal migration may provide clues to our understanding of the enigma of our destiny?

Do monarch butterflies, as the signs of autumn appear, simply begin to experience an overwhelming feeling that compels them to fly off in a certain direction relative to the angle of the sun? Are they guided to their wintering grounds by a powerful destiny field? Is there an external mind overseeing the destiny of this planet? What other clues can we find?

While the migration of the monarch is an astounding journey over vastly differing terrain by a relatively small insect, there are many other examples in nature which equally amaze biologists. Consider the behaviour of European cuckoos. Cuckoos are well known for the fact that they lay their eggs in other birds' nests. The young are hatched and reared by birds of other species, and never see their parents. Towards the end of the summer, the adult cuckoos migrate to their winter habitat in southern Africa. About a month later, the young cuckoos congregate together and then they also migrate to the appropriate region of Africa where they join their elders.[4] How do these young birds, many of which have been raised by non-migrating birds, know how to migrate? How do they know when to migrate and when to reorganise with other young cuckoos? How do they know in which direction they should fly and where their destination is?

Phenomena such as these are so common that we take for granted that scientists know how animals can do such marvellous things, when in fact these remain mysteries that science cannot explain. For example, consider how spiders are able to spin complex webs to the pattern appropriate to their species without learning from other spiders. There are numerous other examples in the fascinating book *Animal Architecture*.[5] In fact, the problem of how the animals 'know' is so widespread that Dr Rupert Sheldrake, a former research fellow at Cambridge University and Director of Studies in biochemistry and cell biology from 1967 to 1973, has suggested that the universe and all its creatures are dominated by a biological *field* which is responsible for, among other things, the instinctive behaviour in animals.[6]

We have discovered that every organism on this planet is characterised by its own unique DNA, which encodes all the genetic information for that species. This information determines the colour of the skin and eyes, the number of legs and so on right down to the minute details of various organs. We have also discovered that every cell in an organism, whether it be a skin cell, an eye cell, a bone cell or a liver cell, contains this unique DNA code.

This property of life is utilised in the practice of tissue culture in agriculture, where the tip of the shoot of a young plant is cut off and placed in a growth medium to grow a stem and root system and thus form a new plant identical to the original. This growth is explained by the fact that the cells in the tip of the plant contain all the genetic information (DNA) for the *whole* plant.

The puzzle remains, however, over how a leaf cell 'knows' that is has to begin to divide into the different types of cells to form a stem, while other cells 'know' to divide to form root cells? Given that a plant has an array of different types of cells making up the various components of a leaf, a stem or a root, how is the overall process of cell division directed so that a complete plant is formed? Similarly, how are the cells that form by the division of a fertilised egg directed to form the various structures—brain, heart, liver, eyes, bones, skin and so on and the connective nerves and tissues—in just the right positions to make up the whole functioning live animal? This phenomenon, which is known as biological morphogenesis, is still a mystery and at present cannot be explained rigorously by any known scientific mechanism.

An enormous gulf of ignorance lies between established facts of molecular biology, biochemistry and genetics. The commonly given explanations for the problem of morphogenesis and why they are inadequate are discussed by Sheldrake.[7]

Here we have an example that fits the interpretation of a biological field produced by an external intelligence which directs the activity of the cells to fulfil a preordained destiny—to arrange themselves in such a way as to grow into a complete plant or animal. There is also evidence for destiny fields at an atomic level.

For example, calcium atoms contain two outer electrons which are in a way 'coupled'. If we alter the spin of one electron the laws of physics require that the spin of the other electron automatically adjusts so that the two electrons are still in 'balance' or 'coupled'. If we excite these electrons and cause them each to emit a particle of light (called a photon) then these photons are also 'coupled'. Physicists have found that even when these particles of light are separated, altering the direction of one photon *instantaneously* affects the direction of the other photon. How this can happen is a mystery to scientists. If both photons are travelling away from each other at the speed of light, how could there be any form of communication that could catch up with the particles and affect them? A communication travelling at more than twice the speed of light would be required. All known forms of electromagnetic radiation, light, radio waves, X-rays and so on, travel at the speed of light. Yet these twin light particles separated in time and space are still somehow interconnected so that the action of one affects the other even though no *known* signal has passed between them.

In the 1930s, when the possibility was first suggested by physicists that one atomic particle could affect another system so far apart that a light signal could not connect them, Einstein ridiculed the notion calling such influences 'spooky' and 'telepathic'. However, in 1982 the effect was demonstrated by Dr Alain Aspect and co-workers in Paris, in an experiment that was widely hailed as one of the most decisive tests of the foundations of modern physics ever made.[8]

The co-ordination of the interference patterns produced by beams of particles such as electrons or photons is similarly extraordinary. When a beam of light is aimed at a screen with two tiny pinholes or slits next to one another, some of the particles of light or photons will strike the screen while others will find their way through the holes. If a second screen or detector is placed behind the holes the light particles that passed through the holes in the first screen will strike the second screen forming many patches of light and dark known as an 'interference pattern'. This phenomena is often demonstrated in college or university physics classes.

When one of the slits is blocked off, the average behaviour of the photons changes dramatically, the interference pattern disappears and, instead, a single bright patch of light is formed on the screen opposite the pinhole. Nor can the interference pattern be constructed by superimposing the patterns produced by two single slits. The interference pattern presents itself only when both apertures are open simultaneously. Now twin-slit interference patterns are not a problem for science to explain if light behaves as a wave, since similar interference patterns can be produced by waves in water. However, scientists were shocked when it was observed that electrons, long established as particles, also produced interference effects.[9]

Even heavy atomic particles such as neutrons, when subjected to the twin slit experiment, were observed to produce an interference-type distribution on the detector.[10] How this can occur is another mystery for scientists. If a neutron can only pass through one slit, how can it 'know' whether or not there is another slit open and therefore position itself on the screen to form an interference pattern as opposed to a single slit patch pattern? Another way of understanding this effect is to imagine that the two slits from the top of a pop-up toaster have been fitted to a kitchen table. If we stand on the table and drop slices of toast, some of the slices will go through the slits and fall in a pattern on the floor beneath. Now if the toast and the slits were the size of atomic particles, we would find that covering just one of the slits would completely change the type of pattern formed on the floor. As theoretical physicist Dr P Davies and his co-author BBC radio producer J Brown write:

> Each photon or electron must somehow *individually* take account of whether both or only one hole is open. But how can they do this if they are indivisible particles? On the face of it, each particle can only go through one slit. Yet somehow the particle 'knows' about the other slit. How?[11]

Some scientists believe that the particles must in some way go through both slits.[12] However, Dr David Bohm, former Professor of Theoretical Physics at Birkbeck College in London and an acknowledged world authority on this branch of physics, has proposed the existence of a special field that affects the reactions of atomic particles relative to their environment. This field, referred to as the 'quantum potential' or 'pilot wave', contains 'active information' which is believed to bring about the quality of 'wholeness' to a system, so that each part of a system moves in a way which reflects the state of the whole.[13] Thus a single electron or neutron would be connected to the twin-slit experiment system and thereby 'know' whether there were one or two holes open.

Bohm proposed that this field is different from the other known fields of physics and acts instantaneously; that is, it is not limited to the speed of light as are the other fields of physics. Bohm proposed that the entire universe was connected by this field, which he called the 'super quantum potential'.[14]

In many ways Bohm's idea of a universal field of 'active information' which co-ordinates the activity of atomic particles is similar to Sheldrake's concept of morphogenic fields that seem to co-ordinate the biological systems of nature. Are these two views in fact describing the application of destiny fields to different aspects of nature?

The idea that a holistic order in the universe which is outside the limits of time and space as we know it has attracted other researchers. The Swiss psychoanalyst Dr Carl Jung and the Austrian theoretical physicist Dr Wolfgang Pauli, who won the 1945 Nobel Prize in physics, proposed a destiny-type connecting principle which they called 'synchronicity'. They compiled evidence for a sort of pervasive field in which apparently independent events occur in conjunction in a meaningful way. Typical of such events are documented instances of extraordinary coincidences, well beyond the expectations of chance.[15] These sorts of coincidences appear to have played a role in determining the course of history. The American philosopher William Hasker describes a 'providential' example in his well-argued book *God, Time, and Knowledge*:

> In a famous World War II battle the Allied armies were encircled by the Germans at Dunkirk in June 1940. The military balance heavily favoured the Germans, and the situation of the Allied forces was desperate. However, unusually calm weather on the English Channel and a fog that inhibited dive bombing by the Luftwaffe made possible the evacuation by sea of most of the Allied troops with far fewer losses than could have been expected.[16]

Similarly the fate of the famous Spanish Armada which was sent to invade England, admits of a comparable interpretation of 'providence', or the influence of a powerful destiny field. The Spanish admiral who planned the nautical strategy, the Marques de Santa Cruz, died in his sleep on 9 February 1588, just before the Armada was due to sail. The commander appointed to replace him, the Duque de Medina Sidonia, was inexperienced at sea and a poor leader of men. The armada was then delayed by storms. Following this, a series of inappropriate decisions and monstrous strategic blunders meant that the Spanish not only lost their opportunity to capture the English fleet when it was in a vulnerable position but also failed to co-ordinate their land and sea forces. Weather conditions favourable to the English forces subsequently facilitated their decisive naval victory and the invasion of England was averted.[17]

Destiny also seemed to play a decisive role in preventing the Mongol invasion of Japan. In 1274 Kublai Khan amassed a Mongol armada which reached Hakata in the Kyushu region of Japan. The Japanese warriors were no match for the mass formations and longbows used by the Mongols, but an unusually violent storm destroyed most of the Mongol fleet and forced the invaders to retire with extensive losses.

A second Mongol invasion comprised of combined Chinese and Korean forces of more than 140 000 men approached Kyushu in 1281. The Japanese had constructed a seawall designed to obstruct landings of the invading armies, and the defending forces were able to hold their own during the summer months. With the arrival of autumn came the typhoon season and with it another 'divine' wind, or *kamikaze*, which destroyed most of the invading fleet. The Chinese and Korean forces were driven off with tremendous loss of life. Marius B Jansen, Professor of History at Princeton University, noted that the destruction of two invading armies by storms at critical times impressed the Japanese people that their country had been saved by divine intervention, and the story of the *kamikaze* became a national epic.[18]

The Voortrekker Monument in Pretoria, South Africa, tells another amazing story of divine providence. In the early 1830s descendants of the early German, French and Dutch settlers of the Cape needed to find a country that was beyond the reach of the Cape Colony government, a place where they would be able to live in peace and freedom. From 1835 onwards, separate groups of settlers decided to trek to the virtually uninhabited inland by ox wagon and establish new farms. These pioneers were called Voortrekkers.

On 6 February 1838, just two days after signing a peace treaty, Piet Retief, the leader of the Voortrekkers, was murdered by Zulu chief Dingane and a series of massacres of the European settlers followed. In November that year Andries Pretorius was invited to become the new leader of the Voortrekkers in Natal, and immediately he began to reorganise and motivate the pioneers. He made arrangements to take 530 men in 64 ox-drawn wagons and confront Dingane's well-organised Zulu army which numbered about 40 000 men. It seemed an impossible task but the Voortrekkers, who were deeply religious people, decided to make a vow to the God of heaven. In the vow they swore to God that if He granted them victory over the Zulus, they would forever commemorate that day as a day of thanksgiving. It was the vow of a young nation with its back against the wall. The vow was made for the first time on 9 December 1838 and repeated every evening as the wagon train moved inland, up to 15 December. That night a Zulu force of between 12 000 and 15 000 warriors, in regiments each carrying its own colour shield, surrounded the Voortrekkers' wagons which had formed a laager, or circle, next to the Ncome River (later called the Blood River).

The Voortrekkers were afraid that the Zulus would attack during the night, as was their custom, and overwhelm them with their superior numbers. In desperation they put up as many lanterns as possible to enable them to see the enemy. However, during the night a miracle occurred when the laager was blanketed by a very dense mist. This was an extremely unusual event at that time of year, in summertime and in the middle of the dry season. Many Zulus were superstitious about the mist, believing that the ghosts of the Voortrekkers' ancestors were protecting them, and decided not to attack.

The next morning the Zulus advanced on the laager and another miracle took place. In the battle, 530 or so Voortrekkers defeated the fierce Zulu army of more than 12 000 warriors without one Voortrekker being killed. This defeat is astounding when one considers that some time later, in 1879, a Zulu army of nearly 20 000 strong overwhelmed a heavily armed British army column of around 1800 men who were encamped near Isandhlwana. An estimated 1400 British troops were killed in that attack.[19] The Voortrekkers honoured their vow and up to the present day 16 December each year is a very sacred day of thanksgiving in South Africa.

The coincidences we have just considered are but a few of the multitude of examples that could be drawn upon which seem to suggest the existence of a destiny field directing the overall course of history. This point has also been noted by the eminent scholar Herbert Butterfield, Professor of Modern History at the University of Cambridge, in the 1950s. He wrote:

It is better worldly-wisdom, even when we are only looking for a pictorial representation, to think of history as though an intelligence were moving over the story, taking its bearings afresh after everything men do, and making its decisions as it goes along—sometimes unpredictable and carrying our purposes further than we wanted them to go ... History is like the work

127

of a person in that its course—even in the things that may affect our personal fate and fortunes six months hence—is so unpredictable; while yet there is some fixity in it too, and even when the unpredictable has happened we can go back and account for it retrospectively, we can show that there was organisation in it all the same.[20]

The pieces of the puzzle of the future are now revealing a pattern. In the previous chapters we have noted how people have seen the future in detail or have been warned of future events. University experiments have been conducted that demonstrate the ability to see events in the past, present and future. It has been shown that one mind can communicate directly with another mind. We have noticed that this communication can take place anywhere—the signals appear to be ubiquitous. These phenomena lie outside the known domain of the laws of physics.

We have considered the substantial evidence for a destiny field (or fields) which is also universal and which appears to influence not only 'apparent free will' decisions we make, but also directs the otherwise random behaviour of atomic particles, biological systems and even major events in nature such as storms and fogs. We now need a framework on which to hang the pieces of our puzzle so that we can begin to see the overall picture. In 1986, Dr R S Laura, a former Harvard and Oxford scholar, published a relatively simple model to explain how the future, the past and the present might coexist in such a way as to allow God to transcend time as we know it.

Let us imagine that we take a piece of flat cardboard, perhaps like the back of a notepad, and, holding the cardboard horizontal, we push a large knitting needle through the centre of the cardboard so that the needle stands vertical. Now the stem of this particular needle has previously been painted with a band of blue paint (say, one centimetre wide) and next to that a band of red paint, then a green band, and then a yellow band, so that it has a series of coloured bands along it. We push the needle through the cardboard until the first blue band lines up with the surface.

Now we can pretend that on the surface of this cardboard there lives a creature whose mind can only experience things in the two dimensions of the surface of the cardboard. We ask this creature to describe its experience in the centre of the cardboard, and it reports seeing a blue circle. This creature can only see two dimensions—length and breadth. Imagine now that the needle is pushed down further so that the red band is at the surface, the blue band now being underneath the cardboard. Once again, we ask our two-dimensional creature to report on what is now perceived. Unsurprisingly, the creature reports the experience of a red circle. When asked what happened to the blue circle, the creature replies, 'The blue circle is gone, it is in the past, *it no longer exists*'. The 'blue circle' has not gone out of existence or been swallowed by the past; it simply exists in the third dimension of space separate from the two-dimensional reality of the creature. Similarly, the future, represented by the green and yellow bands, exists but is unknown to the two-dimensional creature. While the third dimension is admittedly transcendent from our creature's point of view, it is none the less real. Laura concludes his essay with the comment:

> If my thesis is at all correct, its heuristic value is worthy of our consideration ... and the concept of prophecy can involve more than the logical contradiction of seeing a future that has not yet happened. If there is truth to theism, then it can at least once again be proclaimed before science as a profound truth about God's place in and beyond the world.[21]

From Laura's model, if the future and the past exist somewhere, we can explain how at times people have seen the future or the past in amazing detail. But how does this come about? If, figuratively speaking, we are the two-dimensional creatures in the model, how can we possibly see into the third dimension and know the future? Let me extend this concept by using a slightly different example.

Let us imagine we are writing a drama. In our mind we picture the story, how it starts, the various subplots that we weave in and out of the main theme and then we visualise the ending, perhaps involving a totally unexpected turn of events. When we have created the story in our mind, we sit down at our personal computer and begin to type. Taking my musings further, let us suppose that by some marvellous process, whatever is showing on the computer screen is created in real life. In our mind we can see the whole story from beginning to end, but only the part that we activate, in this case by typing into the computer, is created.

On the basis of the model I have just described we might consider that the existence of the universe is the result of 'present' thoughts, represented by the current page on the computer screen, of an external intelligence (God), who has created the drama of the ages. The past and future exist in the 'mind' of God, but only the 'present' is activated as the drama proceeds.

Such a hypothesis offers an explanation as to where the past and future exist. The concept of destiny fields would also be accounted for, as this intelligence is actively and intimately involved in sustaining the existence of the universe according to the plot of the drama of ages. This drama is very different from most dramas, however, in that the actors are given the ability to create their own subplots or destinies within the context of the overall story. As the actors make choices they create new mini destiny fields, thus the story is self-generating and full of variety. If mini plots develop which move too far away from the main theme, other actors are impressed by the main destiny field to make choices which generate new 'correcting' subplots which restore the drama to the main theme. We have already noted Professor Butterfield's observation that the unpredictable events of history seem to regulate themselves as though an intelligence were moving over the story. Recently Dr James Lovelock has obtained world recognition for his published philosophy of *Gaia*, in which he argues that the earth with its unique arrangement of atmosphere, oceans, forests, plankton and so forth behaves like a self-regulating living organism. Lovelock describes numerous feedback or self-regulating mechanisms in nature which keep the environment of our planet within certain limits so that life can exist.[22] In the model I have proposed both history and nature are part of the same drama, inextricably inter-connected and under the influence of the same field.

Earlier in this book I referred to the evidence which suggests that the human mind can influence matter or machines.[23] This, in turn, may hint at the very process whereby an external intelligence (God) may transform his thoughts into the being of the universe. The energy which emanates from this *mind* would be imprinted with the patterns of its thoughts to form the ordered processes we observe as the laws of physics and the 'constants' of nature which define them. The arrangements we observe—from the largest galaxies to living cells to atomic particles—would be formed as a result of these limiting values, such as the universal gravitational constant, which serve to constrain the magnitudes of the various forms of energy. If there is any truth in this hypothesis then we would expect to find evidence of an intelligent design in not just some parts but in every part of nature.

This, in fact, appears to be the case. In the early 1900s Professor L J Henderson, then Professor of Biological Chemistry at Harvard University, was so impressed with the amount of evidence for design in biological systems of nature that he wrote the book *The*

Fitness of the Environment.[24] Since that time scientists have continued to be amazed by the evidence of design to the extent that by the late 1970s and early '80s leading astronomers were proposing the idea that the universe possesses many of its extraordinary properties because they are necessary for the existence of life and intelligent observers like ourselves.[25] University of Sussex astronomer J D Barrow and co-author J Silk wrote in their insightful book *The Left Hand of Creation*:

> Our astonishment at some of the striking properties of the universe must be tempered by the realisation that many of them are necessary prerequisites for the existence of intelligent observers.[26]

They go on to comment:

> The fact that the laws of nature barely, but only barely, allow stable stars to exist with planetary systems today is not a circumstance subject to evolutionary variation ... The laws of nature allow atoms to exist, stars to manufacture carbon, and molecules to replicate—but only just.[27]

In the mid-1990s two leading physicists, both specialists in information technology, have argued convincingly that the overwhelming evidence for intelligent design in every aspect of nature points to the existence of an intelligent mind behind the universe. Professor Werner Gitt is the Director of the German Federal Institute of Physics and Technology and in his book *In the Beginning was Information* he demonstrates, using fascinating examples from nature, that living systems require information and that information cannot come about by random processes. Gitt contends that *information* is a fundamental entity on equal footing with matter and energy.[28] Gitt's arguments are supported by Dr Lee

132

Spetner, formerly from Johns Hopkins University. Spetner writes in his book *Not By Chance*:

> Conventional wisdom holds that life arose spontaneously. In the remote past a simple living organism is supposed to have formed by chance out of inert matter. That organism is then supposed to have reproduced and developed into the life of today through random variation shaped by natural selection. Although not yet widely recognised, the discoveries in biology during the past thirty or forty years, together with elementary principles of information theory, have made this view untenable.[29]

An example of research which illustrates this point was the recent announcement by British scientists that it is extremely unlikely the genetic code on DNA arose by chance. Their studies have shown it to be among the best of more than a billion billion possible codes.[30]

The theory of evolution, which is underpinned by the notion of randomness and chance, is a mechanical model for explaining the origin of life and human consciousness. According to the principles of this model, the concept of destiny is meaningless and it is impossible for us to see the future in dreams or precognitive visions. Premonitions are simply feelings or random dreams which, by chance, coincide with some event.[31]

Given this position, and the abundance of evidence that people have seen the future in dreams and experienced accurate premonitions, it is not surprising to discover that there appears to be no publication in the scientific literature which explains how the evolution of the complex biochemical systems found in living organisms might have occurred. Dr Michael Behe, Associate Professor of Biochemistry at Lehigh University in Pennsylvania, describes in his recent book *Darwin's Black Box* how he made a comprehensive search of the biochemistry literature, including leading research journals and university textbooks, under the subject of evolution.[32] He summarises the results of his search as follows:

> Molecular evolution is not based on scientific authority. There is no publication in the scientific literature—in prestigious journals, speciality journals, or books—that describes how molecular evolution of any real, complex, biochemical system either did occur or even might have occurred. There are assertions that such evolution occurred, but absolutely none are supported by pertinent experiments or calculations. Since no one knows molecular evolution by direct experience, and since there is no authority on which to base claims of knowledge, it can truly be said that— like the contention that the Eagles will win the Super Bowl this year—the assertion of Darwinian molecular evolution is merely bluster.[33]

Modern biochemistry research has uncovered the enormous complexity of simple living cells. Dr Behe's point is that no-one at Harvard University, no-one at the National Institute of Health, no member of the National Academy of Sciences, no Nobel Prize winner—no-one at all can give a detailed account of how the cilium, or vision, or blood clotting or any complex biochemical process might have evolved in a Darwinian fashion.[34] But we live on a planet teeming with living complex organisms. All these things got here somehow. If it was not in a Darwinian fashion, then how did it happen? Dr Behe goes on to suggest that if something was not put together gradually then it must have been put together quickly or even suddenly.[35]

This brings us to some fundamental questions: how old is human history? How far back does our past go? Somewhere we have probably learned that life on earth is millions of years old. This view is based mainly on the radioactive dating results for rocks associated with fossils.

Some recent radioactive dating studies suggest, however, that the conclusions scientists have drawn from these results may be unfounded. For example, near the Crinum Mine in north Queensland fossilised wood has been found entombed in a basalt lava flow. Samples of the fossilised wood and the basalt were sent to both the Geochron Laboratories at Cambridge, in Boston, and to the Australian Nuclear Science and Technology Organisation (ANSTO) near Sydney, where they underwent radioactive dating measurements. The results indicated that the wood was about 35 000 years old and the basalt around 45 million years old, yet these ages should have been the same, not millions of years apart.[36]

Sunset Crater, in northern Arizona, is known to be a recent volcano. Indian artefacts and remains are found within the rocks formed by the volcanic eruptions, and tree-ring dating suggests that the last eruption occurred in about the year 1065. Radioactive dating by the potassium argon method, however, dated the eruption as occurring around 210 000 to 230 000 years ago.[37] In Hawaii, the Kaupelehu Flows on the Hualalai volcano are known to have formed between 1800 and 1801. The flows were dated using a variety of different methods on several different mineral and rock inclusions and 12 different ages were obtained ranging from 2960 million years to 140 million years.[38] Again, these ages should be very similar, not thousands of millions of years apart. The authors of the study were unable to satisfactorily explain why the different minerals gave such different ages.

Extensive radioactive dating studies have been made of rocks associated with the formations of the Grand Canyon, which stretches for about 450 kilometres through northern Arizona. This massive natural wonder is up to 1860 metres deep in places yet lava flows at the rim of the Grand Canyon consistently date millions of years older than buried lava flows beneath the sedimentary rock layers that form its walls, thereby creating an incredible contradiction with regard to radioisotopic dating.[39]

Another area where rocks have been extensively studied by radioactive dating methods is the Koongarra uranium deposit 250 kilometres east of Darwin in northern Australia. Using data from uranium, thorium and lead isotopes, different ages ranging from zero million years to 1445 million years have been reported.[40] What is revealing is that the youngest ages, including a 'zero' million value for three samples, were obtained using the more reliable thorium-derived data. A geologist reviewing the results asserts that 'all of these "ages" are geologically meaningless' and '. . . serious questions must be asked about the validity of the fundamental/foundational basis of the U-Th-Pb "dating" method'.[41]

Clearly, the claims that U-Th-Pb radiometric dating have 'proved' the claimed great antiquity of the earth and its fossils must now be re-evaluated. Furthermore, these results suggest that a radically different interpretation of widely publicised radioactive dates for rocks is long overdue, and that the earth is much younger than we have generally been led to believe from these measurements. This view is also held by Dr Paul Giem at Loma Linda University in the United States, who has recently published an 80-page review of radioactive dating results. Dr Giem argues convincingly that the weight of evidence actually favours a short timeframe for life on earth—in the order of thousands of years—not millions of years.[42] There are many other geological examples which suggest that life on earth is relatively recent, in the order of thousands of years not millions or billions of years, and these have been summarised recently by the American geologist Dr J D Morris.[43]

The belief that life on earth was created only thousands of years ago seems to be supported by the multitude of creation and universal flood traditions around the world. Professor D Leeming, Emeritus Professor of English and Comparative Literature at the University of Connecticut, and co-researcher M Leeming report that many of these stories describe how the world resulted from the 'thoughts' of a creator being. Ancient Hebrew, Egyptian, Hindu, Buddhist, Persian and Mayan cultures, Aboriginal people of northern Australia and many Native American nations held this view. Stories of a massive worldwide catastrophic event from which only a few people survived come from cultures as far apart as the Arandan Aboriginal people of northern Australia, Native American nations of North America, tribes in Africa, China and, of course, ancient Mesopotamia.[44]

When the US Congress commissioned the most comprehensive survey of the Native American tribes of North America in 1847, the historian H R Schoolcraft found that stories of a great deluge from which only a few persons were saved were particularly widespread among the traditions of the tribes.[45] Deluge stories also abound on all levels of Chinese tradition, while ancient Hebrew texts suggest that the Flood occurred sometime during the third millennium BC.[46]

It is curious how records in ancient civilisations appear to go back to about the third millennium BC and then suddenly become very scanty. For example, the first dynasty in China is recorded as beginning in 2205 BC with Chinese legendary history being traced back to the first year of the ruler Huang Ti in 2697 BC.[47] Huang Ti was said to have been the first to clear the hills and plains of bush and wild animals, so that domesticated animals such as cattle could be bred and farmed.[48] Ancient Egyptian chronology prior to the second millennium BC is highly uncertain, with conventional chronologies dating the foundation of the Egyptian state as occurring around 3050 BC.[49] However, a number of leading British archaeologists have argued that periods of conventional Egyptian dating should be shortened by several centuries,[50] which puts the beginnings of Egypt at about the same time as the settlement of China.

Evidence of the existence of another ancient civilisation around this time has been found at Ur, approximately 225 kilometres south of Babylon. Here, a vast cemetery dated about 2700 BC has been discovered, predating the first known Egyptian dynasty. Tombs were uncovered which contained almost incredible treasures in gold, silver, bronze and semiprecious stones. Artefacts including golden weapons, engraved plaques, mosaic pictures, statues, carved cylinder seals and metal reliefs indicating a highly developed civilisation were uncovered.[51]

The many common features of the worldwide ancient creation and flood traditions suggest that they are describing true events which actually occurred in the period just prior to the beginnings of the civilisations mentioned here. Was this knowledge passed down from generation to generation, or were the events seen as a retrocognitive vision by the seers of ancient cultures?

The particularly detailed account in Genesis is believed to have been written by the Hebrew prophet Moses in about 1500 BC, at least 1000 years after the flood it describes. That such detail was preserved in oral traditions is remarkable and it may be more reasonable to assume that Moses received the details of the past by a vision or revelation, as these awesome events would have generated particularly strong destiny fields. The variations in the origins of accounts from various parts of the world may have resulted not only from oral transmission errors and cultural modifications but may also reflect errors or non-aligned data in the impression or vision of the past. In earlier chapters we examined the variations in the premonitions regarding the sinking of the *Titanic* and similar examples of non-aligned data were reported by the Princeton precognition researchers.

A particularly clear example of this sort of precognition error was reported in a biography of the American author Mark Twain, published just two years after his death. As a young man of 20 years, Twain (whose real name was Samuel Clemens) had an extraordinarily vivid dream in which he saw his brother Henry's corpse lying in a metallic burial case supported by two chairs in the sitting room of his sister's house in St Louis. On Henry's breast lay a bouquet of flowers, with a single crimson bloom in the centre. The next morning, Twain confided the details of his dream to his sister.

Mark and Henry had been staying at their sister's home while working on a Mississippi riverboat running between St Louis and New Orleans. A few weeks later the brothers separated in New Orleans and returned on different ships. Four boilers of the paddle steamer *Pennsylvania*, the ship Henry was travelling on, blew up with an enormous loss of life. Henry was badly injured and died several days later in Memphis, Tennessee. Although most of the victims of this disaster were buried in simple wooden coffins, some women in Memphis had been moved by the terrible suffering of Henry Clemens and arranged for a metal coffin for him. When Mark Twain went to see his brother's body, he found it laid out with the others in a metal coffin just as he had seen in his dream, but without any bouquet of flowers. As he stood by the coffin, a lady entered the room and placed on the breast of Henry's body a bouquet of white flowers with one red rose in the centre.[52]

This vivid precognitive dream was highly accurate except for one detail. In the dream Twain saw Henry's coffin in his sister's house in St Louis whereas later Twain actually saw the coffin in Memphis. This could be explained by the details of the future changing in the meantime, making the vision no longer totally accurate. An alternative interpretation, which I prefer, is that the signal of the future which his mind received was poorly resolved in terms of the details of the location of the coffin. In his sleep, Twain's mind may have constructed a location which was familiar to him, his sister's sitting room, to complete the vision.

Another case which would seem to support this hypothesis is the typical remote viewing example involving the California Police Commissioner Pat Price. Price correctly described a park-like area containing two pools of water. But it seems the image was insufficiently clear for him to identify them as swimming pools. Did his mind search for information already on file in his brain to complete the construction of the image, with the result that he described a water treatment plant with extra tanks which were not present at the target site? The evidence that some precognitive visions and dreams are at times not clearly resolved or completely accurate may constitute an important clue about the construction of the future and the past.

The eminent theoretical physicist Professor David Bohm, in his much acclaimed book *Wholeness and the Implicate Order*, introduces the fascinating notion that every part of nature contains enfolded within itself an order or blueprint which reflects the totality of the universe—both matter and consciousness.[53] Bohm refers to this property of existence as the *implicate order* and draws an analogy between this order and the properties of a hologram. Some readers may be familiar with the holographic three-dimensional images produced by laser beams at rock concerts and museums. Life-like images of light are formed when laser beams are reflected off a holographic plate referred to as a hologram, and holographic television and videos are currently being developed.[54]

The hologram or holographic slide is produced by reflecting laser beams off a scene onto a photographic plate. The beams of light carry all the information about the picture and store it as a very complex interference pattern on the plate. In this way a hologram is very different from a normal photographic slide, in that the human eye cannot recognise any details of the original scene by looking at the holographic plate. The image can only be unscrambled using laser beams. However, holograms have a fascinating property. Every *part* of the hologram contains encoded information about the *whole* picture.

Let us imagine taking a 35-mm photographic slide of a swan on a pond. We put the slide in a projector, switch it on and the picture of the swan appears on the screen. If we take a narrow beam of light, say, 1 millimetre in diameter, and direct it to pass through the head portion of the swan on the slide, we will see only the head of the swan projected onto the screen. Let us now imagine making a hologram of the swan on the pond. To view it we beam a laser onto the plate and a three-dimensional representation of the swan is formed. If we now take a tiny laser beam and direct it onto a small part of the holographic plate, a three-dimensional image of the whole swan is still formed although the detail is poorly resolved. For example, it may now be difficult to identify what type of bird it is. This is the unique property of the hologram. Information about the *whole* image is stored on every *part* of the plate.[55] Illumination of only a small portion of the plate still produces the whole picture, but it will be lacking in resolution.

This property of a hologram, whereby a partly illuminated slide produces a poorly resolved image hints at an explanation of the poor resolution that is often associated with precognition and remote viewing or telepathic experiences. Is the universe a hologram? Do the dreams that reveal the future and precognitive visions involve holographic processes? Can a holographic model explain the existence of the past, the present and the future?

Leading brain researcher Dr Karl Pribram from Stanford University, author of the classic textbook *Languages of the Brain*, proposed in 1969 that the brain actually employs a holographic process to structure the data it receives from the five senses.[56] In the early 1980s, consciousness researcher Ken Wilber collated the accumulating evidence supporting Bohm's and Pribram's ideas that a holographic theory could explain a number of puzzling observations not only in physics but in the area of consciousness and brain function. He published his findings as the fascinating book *The Holographic Paradigm and Other Paradoxes: Exploring the Leading Edge of Science*.[57] In 1985 Dr Stanislav Grof, Assistant Professor of Psychiatry at the Johns Hopkins University School of Medicine, also published an accumulation of evidence for a holographic explanation for experiences of the mind.[58]

As we consider the total picture in the light of the evidence discussed in this chapter, could it be that the universe is a hologram of the thoughts of an external intelligence—the creator? Is the image produced by this hologram, from our perspective, human consciousness? Is the human mind a partly illuminated image of the mind of the 'Author of the drama of the ages'? Is this the mechanism whereby we can know the future and the past?

What is presented in this chapter is a heuristic or teaching aid that might explain the phenomena of premonitions and precognition, and that offers a whole new framework for the interpretation of scientific data. I have also outlined new findings which challenge many established doctrines within the area of science such as the Darwinian theory of evolution, the interpretation of radioactive dating measurements and the chronologies of some ancient histories. It has been my purpose to alert readers to the new developments in these areas that, when combined, suggest a coherent picture of the past which is radically different from that proffered by conventional science.

One of the tacit *assumptions* underpinning all science is that the future resembles the past. If a scientist did not *believe* that the future resembled the past there would be no point in carrying out experiments, as one would have no way of connecting the results of one experiment with the results of another. In this sense, having the correct understanding of our past is fundamental to our knowing the future. In this context I have endeavoured to show, in the brief space that I have available for the task, the evidence from leading researchers that gives support to many of the ancient traditions. In particular, the ancient Hebrew traditions seem to provide not only some of the best data about the past, but also evidence for the existence of an intelligent creator who is intimately involved with the destiny of humankind.

In our present age many people still have an intuition that there is a Divine Being behind our existence. The prestigious science journal *Nature*, in April 1997, published a survey revealing that 39.3 per cent of American scientists believe in a personal God they can pray to.[59] In 1998, an Australian-wide survey carried out by a Sydney Sunday newspaper found that about 66 per cent of Australian adults believe in 'God'. The same survey also questioned people about their dreams. The results showed that 39 per cent of people over 18 years of age believed that dreams can predict the future, with 16 per cent of those contacted reporting that they had actually experienced a dream that came true.[60]

Given that the experience of predictive dreams is relatively widespread, what evidence is there of dreams that have revealed the future of this world? This intriguing question is addressed in the next chapter.

Chapter Five

The Millennium Principle: Prophecies and Time Cycles

Of all the prophetic dream records of history, one stands out as spanning from ancient times to the end of our age. It was dreamt by one of the greatest kings of the ancient world, Nebuchadnezzar II. It was this king who built the Hanging Gardens of Babylon, one of the Seven Wonders of the Ancient World, for the enjoyment of his wife, Amytis. He also completed the rebuilding of the famous ziggurat of Babylon. This eminently wise monarch who reigned for 44 years made Babylon not only the most powerful empire of the then known world, but also the centre of learning, particularly in the areas of astronomy, mathematics, astrology and architecture.

One night in the second year of his reign, about 603 BC, Nebuchadnezzar had a particularly vivid dream that troubled him greatly. He could not sleep after this and commanded that the wise men and astrologers of the city be brought to him to interpret the dream. Nebuchadnezzar's advisers did not see a difficulty with this request because Babylonian schools taught dream interpretation. Their confidence, however, was short-lived. Nebuchadnezzar knew the dream was highly significant and was concerned to have the correct interpretation. He therefore, in his wisdom, told his advisers that they must tell him the details of his dream. In this way he would know that the wise men and astrologers would be qualified to tell him the interpretation of his dream. His advisers protested that it was an impossible thing that he was asking. This angered Nebuchadnezzar, and he became furious, ordering that all the wise men of Babylon be killed.

There was in Babylon at that time a number of young Hebrew

captives, whose natural intellectual ability had been noted and as a result they had been sent to the Babylonian schools of learning to be trained as wise men. They also were included under the death decree. One particularly gifted young Hebrew man, by the name of Daniel, obtained an audience with Nebuchadnezzar and successfully gained an extension of time for himself and the other wise men.

Then Daniel went to his house and with several of his closest Hebrew friends prayed to the God of heaven that the mystery of the dream might be revealed to them so that they might not perish. That night Daniel received a vision of the dream together with its interpretation and the next day was taken to the king.

Daniel told the king that the God of heaven had made known to Nebuchadnezzar what would happen in the future. Daniel went on to describe the dream. While in his bed, the king had seen a bright and frightening image. The head of this image was made of finest gold, the chest and arms were made of silver, the belly and thighs were made of bronze, its legs of iron and its feet partly of iron and clay. As the king watched, a stone was cut out by no human hand and hurled at the image. It struck the feet of iron and clay, breaking them in pieces. The rest of the statue collapsed, breaking into pieces as fine as chaff, which were blown away by the wind so that no trace of them could be found. The stone that had struck the image then became a great mountain and filled the whole earth.[1]

Daniel continued with the interpretation as it had been revealed to him. The head of gold represented Nebuchadnezzar and his empire. After him would arise another kingdom inferior to his (the silver chest and arms) and after that a third kingdom (represented by the bronze belly) would rule the world. There would then be a fourth kingdom, as strong as iron, that would break and crush the previous kingdom.

The feet and toes of iron and clay mixed together represented a divided kingdom. Partly strong and partly brittle, its destiny was to become many kingdoms. Some of the kings would try to consolidate their kingdoms through marriage, but just as iron does not mix with clay, these alliances would disintegrate. In the days of these kings, Daniel saw that the God of heaven would put an end to all the kingdoms of the earth—their fate was utter destruction. In their place God would establish His everlasting kingdom.[2]

Nebuchadnezzar was astounded and fell on his face before Daniel, who remained in the king's court. He was later honoured with many gifts and the king made him ruler over the province of Babylon.[3]

The dream of Nebuchadnezzar has amazed scholars for centuries as it accurately describes the course of western history up to the present. Nebuchadnezzar died in 562 BC and his successors were short-lived and insignificant. In 539 BC Babylon fell to the Persian forces led by Cyrus the Great, who, as Cyrus II, became the first ruler of the mighty Persian empire, fittingly represented in Nebuchadnezzar's dream by the chest and arms of silver. Persia eventually controlled a considerably larger territory than Babylon but, as silver is inferior to gold, this second great world empire never equalled its predecessor in splendour and magnificence. Persia ruled the world scene from 539 BC until its conquest, in turn, by Alexander the Great at a battle near Arbela in 331 BC a little more than two centuries later.

History records that the rule of Alexander extended over Macedonia, Greece and the Persian empire, including Egypt, and extended eastward to India. It was the most extensive empire of the ancient world up to that time. The Greek empire was also associated with bronze. The Greek soldiers were noted for their brazen armour; their helmets, shields and battleaxes were made of brass. The historian Herodotus wrote that Psamtik I of Egypt saw in invading Greek pirates the fulfilment of an oracle that foretold men of bronze coming from the sea.[4] The Greek 'world' empire was conquered by the Romans, although in this case the transition was more gradual.

It is revealing to note that later in his life, Daniel himself had a number of visions of the future. One of these occurred while he was serving Belshazzar, the crown prince who was entrusted with royal power during the reign of the last Babylonian king, Nabonidus. In this vision Daniel saw a ram with two horns charging westward, northward and southward from the River Ulai near Susa, in Persia. No other beast could stand before this ram and he did what he pleased. Then Daniel saw in the vision a he-goat coming from the west across the earth without touching the ground. The he-goat had a conspicuous horn between its eyes. He came at the ram with great fury, struck the ram, breaking both the ram's horns. The he-goat cast the ram to the ground and trampled upon him. The he-goat magnified himself exceedingly, but when he was strong, the great horn was broken and instead of it there came up four conspicuous horns pointing towards the four winds of heaven.[5]

Daniel was pondering over what the vision meant when he heard a voice say, 'Gabriel, make this man understand the vision'. An angel appeared and told Daniel that the vision pertained to the future. The ram with the two horns represented the kings of Media and Persia and the he-goat the king of Grecia. The great horn between the eyes was the first king. Four kingdoms would arise from his empire but not with his power.[6]

This vision of the future was fulfilled in detail. The Medes and Persians took over the Babylonian empire and became the dominant power for more than two centuries. Then Alexander the Great, following the assassination of his father Phillip II of Macedonia in 336 BC, succeeded in conquering the entire Persian Empire within five years. But his glory was short-lived. Eight years later, in 323 BC, Alexander died in Babylon at 33 years of age from 'swamp fever' (possibly malaria) after a banquet and bout of heavy drinking in the former palace of Nebuchadnezzar.

After Alexander's death, his generals struggled among themselves for control of the empire. The issue was finally settled at the Battle of Ipsus in 301 BC, and four kingdoms emerged under Lysimachus, Ptolemy, Cassander and Seleucus.[7]

The end of the Greek empire may be thought of as beginning with the Battle of Pydna in 168 BC, when Rome terminated the Macedonian monarchy, or 22 years later when it annexed Macedonia outright. In 64 BC Rome conquered the Seleucid kingdom, which extended from the Aegean Sea eastward almost to the Indus River, and in 30 BC Egypt came under its power. The transition from Greek to Roman power was now complete, and all the major fragments of the extensive empire of Alexander the Great became Roman provinces.

Iron was an appropriate symbol for the Roman Empire in Nebuchadnezzar's dream. Its famed legions ranged at will over the entire Mediterranean world as well as over practically all of western Europe and much of western Asia. As foretold in the dream, Rome literally crushed all other nations. In his *History of the Decline and Fall of the Roman Empire*, the famed English historian Edward Gibbon wrote:

> The arms of the republic, sometimes vanquished in battle, always victorious in war, advanced with rapid steps to the Euphrates, the Danube, the Rhine and the Ocean; and the images of gold, or silver, or brass, that might serve to represent the nations and their kings, were successively broken by the *iron* monarchy of Rome.[8]

By the second century AD the Roman Empire extended from Britain in the west to the Euphrates River in the east and from

Germany in the north to the Sahara in the south, forming the largest and strongest empire the world had ever known. It is fascinating that the prophecy did not foretell of another still greater empire to be built upon the ruins of ancient Rome. Instead, Daniel was shown that the feet of iron and clay in Nebuchadnezzar's dream meant that the empire of iron would be divided into lesser kingdoms whose fragments could never again be permanently reunited. This political situation would continue until God put an end to the nations of the earth and established his own kingdom in their place.

History tells us that the Roman Empire gradually succumbed to successive waves of barbarian invaders. In AD476, the Heruli deposed the last Roman emperor, Romulus Augustus, and over the next century and a half the barbarian attacks continued until the process of inundation was complete. Today, after nearly a millennium and a half, the grand empire that was Rome remains divided exactly as foretold in the dream.

Daniel was also shown that the rulers of these lesser kingdoms would 'mix' with one another 'in marriage' in an endeavour to achieve unity but still would be unable to hold together. Down through the centuries, repeated attempts have been made to unify the nations of Europe both through intermarriage and by military might, but never with more than temporary success. Charlemagne set out to try in about 800, Charles V of Spain in about 1520 and Napoleon Bonaparte in about 1800. Kaiser Wilhelm II's pursuit of a similar ambition led to the First World War and that of Adolf Hitler to the Second World War. In each case, destiny seemed to ensure that their successes were relatively short-lived. Thus the Babylonian king's dream accurately revealed the future of the west to the present time. Will the destruction of the nations and the setting up of God's kingdom also come to pass—possibly in the near future?

The detailed accuracy of the events foretold by Nebuchadnez-zar's dream have led some scholars to believe that the Book of Daniel must have been written after some of the events had happened and was the work of an unknown author during the Helle-nistic era, about 150 BC.[9] However, unexpected archaeological finds during the past century have shed new light on the authen-ticity of Daniel's writings. According to Daniel, Nebuchadnezzar was the great builder of Babylon. Yet the Greek historians never referred to Nebuchadnezzar as a great builder or as the creator of a new and greater Babylon. This honour is usually ascribed to Queen Semiramis, who is given a prominent place in the history of Babylonia, together with another queen, Nitocris.[10] Since the nineteenth century, archaeologists have unearthed cuneiform records from Babylon that corroborate the account in the Book of Daniel crediting Nebuchadnezzar with the rebuilding of 'this great Babylon'.[11] Given that this information had been completely lost by the time of the Hellenistic era, the book was most probably written during the sixth century BC. Further evidence for the accu-racy of the Book of Daniel comes from its mention of a Babylonian king by the name of Belshazzar.

Many readers would be familiar with the expression 'the writing is on the wall', meaning 'it is obvious that such and such is going to happen', which derives from the story of this king. Daniel records how Belshazzar put on a great feast for 'a thousand of his lords'. As the night progressed and the wine flowed freely, the king ordered that the golden and silver vessels taken from the Jewish Temple in Jerusalem by Nebuchadnezzar be brought to the party. As the revellers drank from the vessels, a man's fingers appeared and wrote on the plastered wall of Belshazzar's palace. The king and the guests were horrified. They could not interpret what had been written and neither could any of the astrologers or wise men in the palace. Then Daniel, who was now quite old, was called to the palace. He told the king that the writing was from God, 'the Most High God' who rules the kingdom of men and sets over it whom he will. The interpretation of the words written on the wall was that God had numbered the days of Belshazzar's kingdom and brought it to an end. The king had been weighed in the balances and found wanting. The kingdom was given to the Medes and Persians.[12] Daniel goes on to record that Belshazzar was slain that very night.

Up until the nineteenth century the name of this king had not been found in any writings outside the Book of Daniel, and some scholars doubted the historical accuracy of the account. However, since the 1860s a large number of cuneiform texts have been discovered which confirm that Belshazzar, as a co-regent with his father, Nabonidus, was the king of Babylon at the time when the Persian general Gobryas took the city without resistance on 12 October 539 BC.[13] It is revealing that the ancient Greek historian Xenophon declared 'the impious king' of Babylon, whose name is not mentioned in the account, was slain beside his throne in the banquet hall when Gobryas entered the palace. Xenophon also related that the night the Persians took the city 'a certain festival had come round in Babylon, during which all Babylon was accustomed to drink and revel all night long'.[14]

The account of Belshazzar's feast lends powerful support to the view that God is in overall control of the affairs of humankind. While we have free will, the choices we make reveal our character which sets the foundation for the direction we would choose to take for the course of our lives, if the forces of destiny did not intervene.

Belshazzar revealed his character in that, with the Persian army close at hand, he went ahead with an extravagant and wild party for courtiers. According to Daniel, the young king also showed contempt for the Most High God of heaven by using sacred vessels from the temple for his party.[15]

Daniel then introduces the concept of judgement; the king had been weighed in the balance and found wanting. The theme of a future judgement for mankind permeates the Book of Daniel;[16] in fact the name Daniel in Hebrew means 'God is judge'.[17]

Belshazzar was warned of the impending judgement by the 'writing on the wall' but he ignored its significance and instead proudly and arrogantly proclaimed that he would make Daniel the third ruler in the kingdom.[18] (It is significant that Daniel was to be appointed the 'third' ruler in the kingdom. Only in modern times was it discovered that Belshazzar was the second ruler of the kingdom, as co-regent with his father Nabonidus.)

The young ruler did not believe that the powerful and immensely fortified city could be taken from him. He was totally oblivious of the fact that at that very moment, Persian soldiers were finding their way under the city walls via drained river canals, and that the city would be taken in a single night.[19]

One young monarch who heeded the advice of a dream, according to tradition, was Alexander the Great. The historian Josephus explained that it was because of a dream that Alexander did not destroy Jerusalem during his empire-building campaigns.

In 322 BC, Alexander, flushed with his triumph over Darius at Granicus and Issus, had assumed the role of conqueror and demanded auxiliaries and supplies from the Jews. Jaddua, the high priest in Jerusalem, returned the answer that he was in league with Darius and was resolved to maintain his good faith. Angered by this reply, Alexander vowed that through Jaddua he would show the world with whom it was essential to keep treaty. Upon the fall of Tyre and Gaza, said Josephus, Alexander marched straight for Jerusalem.[20]

When Jaddua heard this he was exceedingly fearful and urged that everyone in Jerusalem should pray to God to deliver them from the 'perils that were coming upon them'. He then had a dream in which he was told to adorn the city and open the gates. The priests were to put on their ceremonial robes and march out, the people of the city following behind dressed in white, to meet Alexander. When Alexander saw the multitude in the distance in white garments, led by the high priest in purple and scarlet clothing with a mitre on his head, he stopped his troops and approached by himself, bowing in adoration to the name of God on the mitre.[21]

Josephus recorded that Alexander's allies were amazed at his behaviour, supposing that he had become disordered in his mind. However, he later explained to them that some years earlier, while at Dios in Macedonia and planning his conquest of Asia he had had a dream in which he saw a person wearing the very same purple and scarlet robes and mitre as the high priest of Jerusalem was wearing. In his dream this person had exhorted Alexander to cross over without delay from Macedonia into Asia with his army and that he would be given dominion over the Persians.[22]

After entering Jerusalem, Alexander was shown the Book of Daniel by Jaddua. Josephus described this meeting of priest and monarch in these words:

And, when the book of Daniel was shown to him [Alexander], in which he had declared that one of the Greeks would destroy the empire of the Persians, he believed himself to be the one indicated; and in his joy he dismissed the multitude for the time being, but on the following day he summoned them again and told them to ask for any gifts which they might desire. When the high priest asked that they might observe their country's laws and in the seventh year be exempt from tribute, he granted all this.[23]

In the passage above Josephus refers to the keeping of the sabbatical year. This practice dates back to the Hebrew prophet Moses, who led the Israelites from captivity in Egypt in about the fifteenth century BC. While worshipping God on Mount Sinai, Moses heard a voice that told him details of a civil code for the newly formed nation of Israel. This code contained rules for conducting worship, for keeping good health, for dealing with crimes and civil offences and for preserving the environment. These laws were later written down as the Third Book of Moses, often called Leviticus.[24]

One of the environmental laws was that orchards could be pruned and fields could be ploughed and sown for six years. But in the seventh year there was to be a Sabbath of solemn rest for the land.[25] That year it was not to be farmed but to lie fallow. What the land itself produced in the Sabbath year could be eaten for food but not harvested or gathered. It was a time for nature to restore the land.

The Jews were particularly keen to be exempt from tribute at this time as it would be difficult to raise the payment if they were not harvesting crops. They were also adamant about keeping this Sabbath of the land as their historians had noted that the 70 years of captivity they experienced from the time of Nebuchadnezzar (around 605 BC) until their release by Cyrus (around 535 BC) was a result of their disobedience in regard to the laws that God had given them through Moses.[26] The 70 years the Jews were kept from their fields meant the land was now enjoying its due Sabbaths.[27] This suggests the Jewish nation had not been keeping the Sabbath of the land for the previous 420 years (that is, for every six years of sowing and reaping, one Sabbath year was due).

Curiously, this time period corresponded very closely with the beginning of the kingdom of Israel under the first king Saul, about 1020 BC.[28] Could it be that the destiny of humankind is linked to cycles of time? Can major events of the future be predicted on the basis of cycles of time? Since Isaac Newton discovered the laws of motion and the law of gravity, scientists have observed that the laws of nature follow mathematical principles and, to some scientists, 'God' must be a mathematician.[29] Does the course of history also follow mathematical patterns? Can the future be predicted using these patterns? Is the Sabbath cycle of rest associated with destiny fields governing humankind? Other revelations and visions experienced by the ancient seer of Babylon suggest that it does.

Sometime after Babylon had been captured by the Persians and a new ruler appointed over the kingdom, Daniel was praying to God in the evening as was his custom. He had been appealing to God that his people might now be allowed to return to their lands when, once again, he was visited by the angel Gabriel. Gabriel told Daniel that God had heard his prayer and that he had been instructed to give Daniel new insight and understanding regarding the earlier vision. Gabriel announced there would be a time of 70 'weeks' of years or 70 seven-year periods (corresponding to 70 Sabbaths of the land) for the people to put an end to sin and to atone for their wickedness. This period of 490 years would span from the time of the issuing of the decree to rebuild Jerusalem until the coming of the 'Anointed One' who would be cut off, thereby putting an end to sacrifice and offering. Then a ruler would come who would destroy the city and the temple.[30]

One of the most recent commentaries on the Book of Daniel has been written by former University of Manchester scholar Dr Desmond Ford who studied under the eminent theologian F F Bruce, Rylands Professor of Biblical Criticism and Exegesis. In his preface to the Book of Daniel, chapter 9, which contains the above prophecy, Ford writes:

Sir Isaac Newton, the greatest of scientists prior to the modern period, wrote a commentary upon the prophecies of Daniel and Revelation. He described [chapter] 9:24–27 as 'the foundation stone of the Christian religion', because centuries in advance it gave the exact time of the appearance of the Messiah and the date of His death, as well as a comprehensive description of His saving work in heaven and earth. The prophecy likewise tells what would be the fate of the Jews consequent upon their rejection of the One whose coming they had long anticipated. The destruction of Jerusalem in AD 70 was history's testimony that the offerings and services of the sanctuary had met their fulfilment in the advent of the promised Messiah.[31]

Ford went on to point out that the decree to rebuild Jerusalem was given by the Persian king Artaxerxes I in 457 BC. After 69 weeks of years, or 69 Sabbaths of the land, had passed, at the beginning of the seventieth week, in AD 27, Jesus the Messiah was anointed.[32]

Daniel was told by the angel that in the middle of this last week of years, the Anointed One, who was to be 'cut off' or suffer the death penalty, would put an end to sacrifice and offering.[33] This prophecy was fulfilled when, at three o'clock on 'black' Friday (now known as 'Good Friday') AD 31, Jesus the Christ was put to death on a Roman cross outside Jerusalem.[34]

It is astounding that such detailed predictions could be made more than five centuries ahead of their fulfilment. Given the impressive 'track record' of the prophecies in the Book of Daniel, we might ask are there any 'Sabbath cycles' relating to the future? Is there another Sabbath or rest period for the earth? What about the period of time depicted by the stone in Nebuchadnezzar's dream?

The last vision recorded in the Book of Daniel may provide some important clues, since it relates to the time of the end. This prophecy, which is quite long, is enigmatic and controversial, and a detailed discussion of the entire prophecy is outside the scope of this book. (However, readers are referred elsewhere for details.)[35] In summary, Daniel was shown in a vision that the current era of earth's history would come to an end as the earth experiences a time of distress such as has never been experienced before by the nations. The people of God whose names are found written in the 'book' (presumably in heaven) are promised deliverance at that time by a great prince 'Michael'. At this time there is a resurrection of the dead, some to everlasting life and some to judgement.[36] In an earlier experience, Daniel had been given a vision of a court sitting in judgement in which the 'books' (of heaven) were opened before the 'Ancient of Days'. After this the 'saints' received the new kingdom of God, which was represented by the stone that smote the image and then filled the whole earth in Nebuchadnezzar's dream.[37]

An identical picture of the future was portrayed in a powerful vision written down by a Jewish writer of the first century AD, who had been condemned to labour in the mines on the island of Patmos in the Aegean Sea by Caesar Domitian (AD81–96).[38] This prophecy, which is known as the Revelation to John, is preserved as the last book of the Bible.

Like Daniel, St John was meditating and praying when he heard a loud voice command him to write down the things he was about to hear and see.[39] The visions he received revolve around the judgement of the peoples of earth by God for the way they have treated each other and the earth. In the central vision of the book, St John writes down words he heard spoken in heaven at about the time of the end:

We give thee thanks, O Lord God, sovereign over all, who art and who wast, because thou hast taken thy great power into thy hands and entered upon thy reign. The nations raged, but thy day of retribution has come. Now is the time for the dead to be judged; now is the time for recompense to thy servants the prophets, to thy dedicated people, and all who honour thy name, both great and small, *the time to destroy those who destroy the earth* [my emphasis].[40]

157

This last phrase carries the connotation of the rape of the earth and of not letting the earth recover and regenerate as in the sabbatical year. That is, one of the reasons why the Jews were taken away from their land was so that it would enjoy the Sabbath of the land and recover.

In one of the latter visions, St John saw a huge multitude of the angels of heaven led by one called 'Faithful and True' wearing a robe inscribed: 'King of kings and Lord of lords, approach the earth and those who had been destroying the earth, the wicked, were slain.'[41] Then St John saw two resurrections of the dead take place 1000 years apart. In the first resurrection were those who had worshipped God in the past and died believing in Him. They lived with God during this 1000-year period. At the end of this time the rest of the dead were raised and judged according to what they had done as recorded 'in the books' of heaven. They then faced a second death, if their name was not found written in the book of life.[42]

These events harmonise perfectly with the visions of Daniel. Could it be that the 1000-year period, which follows the destruction of the 'wicked' (people who have been destroying the earth and each other), constitutes a Sabbath rest for the earth? Is this period a sabbatical 'year' 1000 years long, following the 6000 years that we have been harvesting, mining and polluting the earth? Are we soon to enter a special period in earth's history, the seventh millennium, which will be very different from the previous millennia?

In the previous chapter we noted the archaeological and historical evidence for the existence of advanced civilisations that goes back to the third and possibly the fourth millennium BC and then suddenly vanishes. What happened at that time? Clearly, something significant happened in the history of this planet about 6000 years ago. Was it the flood or creation referred to in the traditions of the various tribes and nations around the world, or was it some other event?

The ancient book Genesis, which contains the account of the dreams of Joseph, describes life on earth being created by an intelligence over six days followed by a day when the earth was to rest and the first created beings were to spend time with the Creator.[43] This basic cycle of a seven-day week, involving six working days and one rest day for worship and recreation, has been preserved by Jewish and Christian tradition to the present day. Could it be that this same 'intelligence' destined humankind to be the steward of this creation for 6000 years and to then spend a 1000 years with the Creator? Are we meant to have a kind of 'sabbatical leave' perhaps learning of other existence realities or visiting other worlds in parallel universes? Is the seventh millennium destined to be a very special time for us?

The concept that the destiny of our planet follows cycles of time is, of course, not new. The ancient Babylonian art of astrology was based on the belief that our destiny was intimately linked to the natural cycles of the planets and stars.

Shirley J Case, Professor of Early Church History at the University of Chicago, points out that the Zoroastrians of Persia believed in 3000-year time cycles. The last cycle began with the appearance of Zoroaster around 630 BC. Zoroaster was thought to have been sent by God to bring the divine revelation to humankind. For Zoroastians, his work marked the beginning of the final 3000-year period which includes modern times and is to close with the catastrophic end of the world when all evil will be annihilated.[44]

Another civilisation that believed in time cycles were the Aztecs. They used the 52-year cycle of the Mayan calendar, and believed that the world would come to an end at the close of one of these 52-year periods.[45] We have discussed how the arrival of Cortez at Tenochtitlan in 1519 coincided with the tenth cycle of a prophecy which predicted the end of the Aztec empire.

Another ancient civilisation that had an absorbing interest in time cycles were the Maya of Central America. Based on the belief that history repeats itself, good days—for a wedding, for beginning a war, for consecration of a ruler, for naming a child and so on— were predicted mathematically by the priests.[46] We noted that the Mayans had developed a highly accurate calendar and chronology system which dates the beginning of time as 3113 BC. This, presumably, was calculated from the date they believed the creation of the current world took place, the previous world having been destroyed by a flood.[47] Details of the Mayan calculations into the past and into the future are given by the scholars J E S Thompson and S G Morley. According to the generally accepted calendrical correlation, the current great cycle will end on Saturday 21 December 2012.[48] Whether time cycles can be used to predict the future or merely serve to demonstrate that there is a blueprint for the destiny of the world is a moot point.

There is convincing evidence that people have seen the future in detail and I have discussed the visions where future events were foretold to Daniel in terms of cycles of time. However, this does not imply that other future events have to be constrained by these time cycles. Some prophecy researchers have argued that the 'intelligence' or 'God' that controls the destiny of the universe has arranged future events to happen when certain time cycles occur so that 'believers' know beforehand when these events will take place. For example, last century, the British theologian and eschatologist H Gratton Guinness, in his fascinating book *Light For the Last Days: A Study Historic and Prophetic*, on the basis of obscure time cycles in the Book of Daniel, calculated that either 1917 or 1923 or possibly 1934 would be significant dates for the Jews.[49] Guinness went on to argue:

The year 1917 is consequently *doubly* indicted as a final crisis date, in which the 'seven times' run out, as measured from two opening events, both of which are clearly most critical in connection with Israel, and whose dates are both absolutely certain and unquestionable.[50]

Guinness uses very strong terms to describe his confidence in this date and in certain respects his confidence has been vindicated. It was in November 1917 that the British government issued the Balfour Declaration which stated that:

His Majesty's Government view with favour the establishment in Palestine of a national home for the Jewish people, and will use their best endeavours to facilitate the achievement of this object . . .[51]

Later that same year British General E H H Allenby captured Jerusalem, ending more than seven centuries of almost unbroken Muslim control of the city. While these events undoubtedly contributed significantly to the later establishment of the state of Israel in 1948, I would not suggest that 1917 constituted a 'final crisis date'.

The dates 1923 and 1934 do not seem to align with any particularly significant events in the history of Israel. It is curious, however, that exactly a Jubilee later, in 1967, Israel obtained full control of Jerusalem after the Six-Day War. The Jubilee was another ancient law, given by God to Moses when he was on Mount Sinai, which required that every 50 years liberty was to be proclaimed throughout the land. All debts were to be cancelled, slaves were to be freed and land which may have been sold was to revert back to the original family that had inherited it.[52] In 1967, ownership of the temple site in Jerusalem was restored to the Jews. It could also be said that the re-establishment of the nation of Israel, from 1917 onwards, took place during the Jubilee of Jubilees; that is, the fiftieth 50-year period after the Jews returned to Jerusalem to restore the first temple at the end of their Babylonian captivity in about 536 BC.

In recent times there has been a renewed interest in prophetic calculations relating to the 'end time' and some popular authors have predicted major events in the history of this planet occurring early next century, on the basis of Jewish and Mayan time cycles.[53] However, do such calculations really help us *know* the future? How can we know which of the predicted dates if any will be correct?

For example, in the early part of last century there was widespread interest by Bible scholars in the prophecies of the Book of Daniel. American clergyman William Miller calculated on the basis of an enigmatic time period given in the eighth chapter of The Book of Daniel and the date of Artaxerxes' decree to rebuild Jerusalem, that Jesus Christ would return in 1843 or 1844. His views were widely published in the late 1830s and early 1840s and led to the Millerite movement involving an estimated 50 000 to 100 000 people who prepared themselves for the 'second coming'.[54]

The fact that Jesus Christ did not return at that time does not necessarily mean that this will not happen, but rather that we cannot with confidence *know* when the prophecy will be fulfilled on the basis of calculating time cycles. In the case of the Millerite movement, their prediction was based on a problematic passage in the Book of Daniel referring to the restoration of the 'sanctuary'.[55] Some scholars, for example, believe this prophecy had already been fulfilled in 165 BC, when the Jewish temple was ceremoniously cleansed and rededicated after a period of desecration by the Greek ruler Antiochus Epiphanes.[56]

There are a large number of possible significant dates for the future of the world that could be calculated from permutations of various time cycles with different historical starting dates. But which date should we link with what possible future event? While we would have hypothesised about the future, when all was said and done we would be no further advanced in terms of *knowing* the future.

It seems that the only way we can truly *know* the future is when it is revealed to us. The historical revelations discussed in this chapter suggest that we are coming to a new era in the history of this planet which will be vastly different from anything in the past.

Chapter Six

Our Future in the Seventh Millennium

The challenge we face when we know the future is how to make the best use of this knowledge. What plans and decisions should we be making now? The preceding chapters present substantial evidence that some people have seen the future in detail, the concept that the future and the past may exist in a holographic form, and some of the visions of the future which predict a vastly different seventh millennium for earth's history. But if the future already exists, how can we have freedom of choice, or 'free will'? If we do not like the future can we change it? Can we change our destiny?

The implications of the apparent inherent contradiction that there is an intelligence or 'God' who knows the future and that we humans have free will has been debated almost endlessly by philosophers and theologians down through the ages.[1] Various explanations for this conundrum have been offered but there is little consensus among experts.[2] A discussion of these often deep philosophical arguments is well outside the scope and intention of this book.

Rarely, however, is the issue of predestination and human freedom of choice presented in the context of the evidence provided by the multitude of dream and vision experiences that have revealed the future. In Mike Martin's dream, why should his wife's car go out of control on the very corner he saw in his dream? As Paul was walking alongside his injured brother, why should the very girl he saw in his dream be standing near the window and wave and smile exactly as he foresaw?

Alexander the Great had a dream where he was told he would

conquer Persia. Could he not have been accidentally killed in battle before he had the chance to conquer Darius's empire? Battles where there is hand-to-hand fighting are chaotic. A few centimetres difference in the swing of a sword, the thrust of a spear or the movement of a shield may mean the difference between life and death in a fast-moving battle. How can an individual's future be known under such conditions when so many split-second choices are being made? Alexander was almost killed during the first encounter with the Persian army at the Battle of Granicus in 334 BC, but his life was saved by the daring action of his cavalry commander Cleitus.[3] Was Alexander's rescue by Cleitus 'providential'? Did Cleitus succeed because Alexander was 'destined' to fulfil his mission?

When Alexander had his dream, he was spoken to by a being dressed like a priest. Daniel, in his visions, saw an 'angel', as did Joan of Arc. Angels were reported at the Battle of Mons and in the story of the little girl kidnapped in Zimbabwe. Many other accounts of the involvement of angels in the affairs of humankind have been recorded.[4] Are angels involved in determining our destiny and fulfilling visions of the future? Do angels make choices that affect our lives? Are there different types of 'angels'?

There are many questions that remain to be answered and much more research needs to be done if we are but to begin to understand the mysteries of our existence. Yet some scientists believe we are on the verge of understanding 'everything'.

In April 1980, one of the world's most eminent scientists, Stephen Hawking, commenced his appointment as Lucasian Professor of Mathematics at Cambridge University. In his inaugural lecture, entitled 'Is the End in Sight for Theoretical Physics?' He began by saying: 'In this lecture I want to discuss the possibility that the goal of theoretical physics might be achieved in the not too distant future, say, by the end of the century. By this I mean that we might have a complete, consistent and unified theory of the physical interactions which would describe all possible observations.'[5]

If we accept Hawking's dictum, it would seem that the ultimate goal of science has almost been achieved. Imagine he is correct. What is it that we have really achieved? Have we perhaps exaggerated the success of contemporary science? Writing in *New Scientist* magazine, social worker Chris Beckett points out that:

> ... When Hawking talks about a theory that would describe the whole Universe, what he actually means is a theory that would describe only a very small corner of it (and not a very important corner either, at least from the human perspective). The unified theory would not help us to resolve the dilemmas with which we struggle in everyday life.[6]

Will science help us to solve the problems of unemployment, crime, violence, the breakdown of family relationships or the tragedy of youth suicide where young people can no longer see a future that is worth living for? Will learning more physics, chemistry and studying evolution, and encouraging unlimited economic growth together with increased efficiency, bring an end to the pollution of our oceans, the erosion of our precious topsoils and the clearing of our last great stands of rainforests? Will we be empowered to not destroy the life support systems of our planet in the name of progress?

The earth badly needs time to rest and recover.[7] The ozone layer needs time to repair itself. Rainforests need time to grow again. Somehow the vanishing topsoils of our planet need to be replenished. Our oceans need time to be detoxified, and fish and mammal stocks allowed to build up. Endangered species need time for re-establishment of their habitats. Will we humans bring about these changes or will 'the Creator' bring about a 'Sabbath year' period for the earth to recover? As stewards of this beautiful planet will we be weighed in the balance and found wanting?

Science has no explanation for how a mother can have a premonition that something has happened to her child; it cannot explain how primitive tribespeople could know what their family members were doing 100 kilometres away; it cannot explain how dogs and other pets can commonly anticipate when their owners are returning home even though they may be keeping extremely irregular hours; it cannot explain how a young woman my wife and I met could, through meditation, call whales from out at sea to come to her and play. Science cannot explain the experiments of remote viewing or precognition where people have seen distant places in detail they have never been to or describe events in the future; it cannot explain why the principles of acupuncture or Feng Shui can work; it cannot explain the experiences of angels or voices that warn of danger, or dreams that show the future in detail. And despite its protestations to the contrary, science cannot explain 'life' or how we came to be here, yet here we are. All this evidence points to a whole dimension of our being which is generally ignored by conventional science—the existence of an intelligent 'Creator'.

For over four millennia, up to the year 1911, the reigning emperors of China performed an annual sacrifice to Shang Ti, the Heavenly Ruler who created the earth. The Temple and Altar of Heaven, T'ien T'an, in Beijing, are today prime tourist attractions. Yet few people in the surging crowds which clamber over the worn marble steps realise that the origin of the 'Great Sacrifice' collaborates the Hebrew Genesis account of the creation of the world.[8] So important to the mind of the sage Confucius (551–479 BC) was this 'Great Sacrifice' that he wrote: 'He who understands the ceremonies of the sacrifices to Heaven and Earth ... would find the government of a kingdom as easy as to look into his palm!'[9]

It is the contention of this book that the future of the world was revealed by the God of heaven, the Creator of the world, to the ancient Babylonian king, Nebuchadnezzar, more than two and a half millennia ago. Since then more details of the future have been revealed in dreams and visions to ancient seers such as Daniel and St John, among others.

There is convincing evidence that the history of this planet is already mapped out from beginning to end. We can choose to create a destiny for ourselves which is in harmony with the divine plan or, alternatively, we can choose to ignore the evidence and create a future based on 'blind' science.

If there is any truth in the tale of the Swaffham tinker then it serves to illustrate my point. The sceptic on London Bridge ignored his dream and went happily on his way, ignorant of the riches he could have had. The Swaffham tinker believed his dream and found the treasure. He thought beyond the reality that he saw and heard and questioned it. He sifted the evidence, looked for the truth and was rewarded. Yet the tinker was an ordinary man of his day. The invitation is still open today to anyone who will pursue authentic interpretations of the signs, visions and dreams that reveal the future. Millions of people over the ages have trodden this path, and those on it now look to the future with confidence.

Endnotes

Introduction

1 J Taylor, *Science and the Supernatural*, Granada, London, 1980, p 83. See also N Bludell, *The Supernatural*, Promotional Reprint Co Ltd, London, 1996, pp 91–96

2 J Taylor, op cit, p 70

3 ibid, p 67

4 ibid, Chapter 10

5 ibid, p 177

6 R G Jahn and B J Dunne, *Margins of Reality*, Harcourt Brace Jovanovich, San Diego, 1988, pp 124–30

7 ibid, p 128

8 See, for example, Q Sherrer *Miracles Happen When You Pray*, Zondervan Publishing House, Grand Rapids, Michigan, 1998

9 A S Maxwell, *Your Bible and You*, The Signs Publishing Company, Warburton, Australia, 1959, pp 176–81

10 B Miller, *George Muller: Man of Faith and Miracles*, Dimension Books, Minneapolis, Minnesota, 1941. See also A S Maxwell, op cit, pp 173–75

11 B Miller, op cit, pp 53–8, 133

12 ibid, p 57

13 ibid, pp 157–8

14 F A Schaeffer, *Pollution and the Death of Man*, Tyndale House Publishers, Wheaton, Illinois, 1981

15 F A Schaeffer, *Death in the City*, Intervarsity Press, Chicago, 1970, pp 115–6

16 ibid, pp 114–5

17 B Carson and C Murphey, *Gifted Hands*, Review and Herald Publishing Association, Washington DC, 1990, pp 152–3

18 H Price, *Angels: True Stories of How they Touch Our Lives*, Macmillan, London, 1993, pp 92–3

19 ibid, pp 93–4

20 ibid, p 93

21 ibid, pp 94–5

22 ibid, pp 96–7

23 J H Randall, *The Making of the Modern Mind*, Houghton Mifflin Co, Boston, 1940, pp 258–60

24 M Gauquelin *Dreams and Illusions of Astrology*, Prometheus Books, Buffalo, New York, 1979, pp 30–1

25 J Oates *Babylon*, Thames and Hudson, London, 1996, pp 178–80

26 Gauquelin, op cit, p 30–1

27 K Thomas, *Religion and the Decline of Magic*, Penguin Books, London, 1984, pp 342–3

28 Gauquelin, op cit, p 12. See also: G Tibbals, *The Titanic: The Extraordinary Story of the Unsinkable Ship*, Reader's Digest Australia, Surry Hills, New South Wales, 1997, pp 12, 51

29 ibid, pp 13–4

30 ibid, p vi

31 ibid, pp 141–53

32 ibid, p 145

33 ibid, p 147

34 ibid, p 153

35 J English, 'A Scientist's Experience with Tarot', in J Wanless and A Arrien (eds), *The Wheel of Tarot; A New Revolution*, Merrill-West Publishers, Carmel, California, 1993

36 C S McCusker and B McCusker, 'An Experimental Test of the Bias of Probability Theory', *Australian Physicist*, Vol 25, No 1, 1988, pp 20–3. See also McCusker B, and Sutherland C, 'Probability and the Psyche', *Journal of the Society for Psychical Research*, (London), Vol 57, January 1991

37 S Morley, *The Ancient Maya*, Stanford University Press, Palo Alto, California, 1956, pp 234–57

Chapter 1

1 R L Van de Castle, *Our Dreaming Mind*, Ballantine Books, New York, 1994, pp 10–11

2 ibid, pp 22–23

3 See M Gandhi, *An Autobiography: The Story of My Experiments With Truth*, Beacon Press, Boston, 1957

4 M Kelsey, *Dreams: The Dark Speech of the Spirit*, Doubleday, New York, 1968, pp 124–6

5 A H M Jones, 'Constantine', in *Encyclopaedia Britannica*, Encyclopaedia Britannica, Inc, Chicago, 1967, vol 6, p 385

6 ibid, pp 385–6

7 Van de Castle, op cit, pp 34

8 R de Becker, *The Understanding of Dreams and Their Influence on the History of Man*, Hawthorn Books, New York, 1968, p 85

9 Van de Castle, op cit, p 35

10 P Davies, *The Mind of God*, Simon & Schuster, London, 1992, pp 153–4

11 ibid p 154

12 B Kedrov, 'On the Question of Scientific Creativity', in *Voprosy Psikologii*, Vol 3, 1957, pp 91–113 (Cited in Van de Castle, op cit, p 35)

13 Van de Castle, op cit, p 35

14 ibid, pp 35–6

15 L Talamonte, *Forbidden Universe*, Stein & Day, New York, 1975

16 M Fagen (ed), *A History of Engineering and Science in the Bell System: National Service in War and Peace (1925–1975)*, Bell Telephone Laboratories, Murry Hill, New York, 1978. See also G Schindler, 'Dreaming of Victory', in *New Scientist*, 31 May 1997, p 53

17 G Hancock, *Fingerprints of the Gods*, Crown Trade Paperbacks, New York, 1995, p 135

18 D K Down, 'The Pyramids of Egypt', in *Archaeological Diggings*, April/May, 1997, pp 3–5. See also I E S Edwards, *The Pyramids of Egypt*, Penguin Books (originally published 1947), and A Cremin (ed), *The Enduring Past*, New South Wales University Press, New South Wales , 1988, pp 18–21

19 J Baines and J Malek, *Atlas of Ancient Egypt*, Time-Life Books, Amsterdam, 1995, p 36

20 C L Woolley, 'Ur', in *Encyclopaedia Britannica*, Encyclopaedia Britannica Inc, Chicago, vol 22, 1967, pp 773–5

Endnotes

21 R J C Atkinson, 'Stonehenge', ibid, vol 21, pp 275–77

22 G S Hawkins, 'Sun, Men and Stones', in *American Scientist*, vol 53, No 4 (December 1965), pp 391–408

23 S Morley, *The Ancient Maya*, Stanford University Press, Palo Alto, California, 1956, pp 256–7

24 Hancock, op cit, p 159

25 W Newbold, 'Sub-Conscious Reasoning', in *Proceedings of the Society for Psychical Research*, vol 12, 1886, pp 11–20 (cited in Van de Castle, op cit, pp 37–8)

26 Van de Castle, op cit, p 38

27 ibid, p 49

28 M Bietak, *Avaris: The Capital of the Hyksos*, British Museum Press, London, 1996. See also M Bietak, 'Egypt and Canaan During the Middle Bronze Age', in *Bulletin of the American Schools of Oriental Research*, vol 281, 1991, pp 27–72

29 H H Rowley, 'Genesis', *Encyclopaedia Britannica*, Encyclopaedia Britannica Inc, Chicago, vol 10, 1967, pp 79–82

30 Genesis, 37–82

31 *The History of Herodotus*, Book1:200, William Benton, Publisher, Chicago, 1952

32 ibid, 209–4

33 ibid, Book III:123–5

34 J C Rolfe, *Suetonius*, William Heineman, London, 1964, pp 109–11

35 W Shakespeare, *Julius Caesar*, Act 2, Scene 2.2, in *The Complete Works* (Compact Edition), Clarendon Press, Oxford, 1988, p 610

36 de Becker, op cit, p 62

37 B Hill, *Gates of Horn and Ivory: An Anthology of Dreams*, Taplinger, New York, 1967, pp 21–2

38 W Lamon, 'Abraham Lincoln's Dream Life', in R L Woods (ed) *The World of Dreams*, Random House, New York, 1947, pp 383–5

39 M Boss, *The Analysis of Dreams*, Philosophical Library, New York, 1958, pp 186–7

40 Van de Castle, op cit, p 29

41 S Wellman, *Corrie Ten Boom, Heroine of Haarlem*, Barbour and Company, Uhrichsville, Ohio, 1995, pp 66, 102

42 Van de Castle, op cit, p 408

43 T White, 'The College', in B Hill (ed) *Such Stuff as Dreams*, Rupert Hart-Davis, London, 1967, pp 9–10

44 S Bradford, *Harriet Tubman: The Moses of Her People*, Peter Smith, Gloucester, Massachusetts, 1981 (cited in Van de Castle, op cit, p 22)

45 Van de Castle, op cit, pp 27–8

46 ibid, pp 21–2. See also E Blomefield, 'The Swaffham Tinker', in R L Woods (ed), *The World of Dreams*, Random House, New York, 1947, pp 378–80

47 L Rhine, *Hidden Channels of the Mind*, Sloane, New York, 1961

48 Van de Castle, op cit, p 409

49 ibid, p 11

Chapter 2

1 See, for example, N Rescher, *Predicting the Future*, State University of New York Press, 1997. See also I Stewart, *Does God Play Dice*, Penguin Books, London, 1990

2 I Stevenson, 'Prediction of Disasters', in *Journal of the American Society of Psychical Research*, vol 64, 1970, pp 187–210

3 I Stevenson, 'Seven More Paranormal Experiences Associated with the Sinking of the Titanic', in *Journal of the American Society of Psychical Research*, vol 59, 1965, pp 211–24

4 G Tiballs, *The Titanic: The Extraordinary Story of the 'Unsinkable' Ship*, Reader's Digest Australia, Surry Hills, New South Wales, 1997, pp 9–12

5 ibid

6 ibid, pp 53–4

7 ibid, pp 12, 82

8 ibid, p 8

9 W G Watt, 'Shipping Routes' in *Encyclopaedia Britannica*, Encyclopaedia Britannica Inc, Chicago, 1967, vol 20, pp 428–9

10 J Cohen, 'That's Amazing, Isn't It?', in *New Scientist*, 17 January 1998, pp 24–8. See also J Cohen and I Stewart, *Figments of Reality*, Cambridge University Press, Cambridge, 1997

11 M Roberston, *The Wreck of the Titan*, Pocket Books, London, 1998 (First publishd as *Futility* in 1898)

12 Tiballs, op cit, p 15

13 ibid, p 19–21

14 'Titanic' Disaster, *Encyclopaedia Britannica*, Encyclopaedia Britannica, Inc, Chicago, 1967, vol 22, p 28

15 Tiballs, op cit, pp 71–2

16 ibid, p 100

17 'Titanic' Disaster, op cit

18 Tiballs, op cit, pp 8–9

19 ibid, p 26

20 ibid, pp 63–70

21 ibid, pp 64–5, 68–70

22 ibid, pp 76, 93, 110, 122

23 M D Berstein, 'Quetzalcoatl', *Encyclopaedia Britanica*, Encyclopaedia Britannica Inc, Chicago, 1967, vol 18, p 961

24 J Glass, *The Story of Fulfilled Prophecy*, Cassell, London, 1969, pp 63–5

25 S de Madariaga, 'Cortes, Hernan', *Encyclopaedia Britannica*, Encyclopaedia Britannica Inc, 1967, vol 6, pp 555–6

26 Luke 21:25–28. See also Matthew 24:3–8 and 27–31, and Mark 13:24–26. Note also reference 27 below. Many commentators believe that the destruction of Jerusalem is a prophetic type of the destruction of all the cities of the world at the second coming of Jesus Christ (*Bible Readings for the Home Circle*, Pacific Press Publishing Association, Mountain View, California, 1935, p 312)

27 Luke 21:5–11

28 Matthew 24:27

29 Matthew 24:30. See also Revelation 1:7

30 Mark 13:27, Matthew 24:31

31 Luke 21:20–21

32 Luke, 21:23–24. See also 19:43–44

33 Matthew 24:1–2. See also Mark 13:1–2, and Luke 21:5–6

34 Matthew 24:21. See Mark 13:19

35 W Keller, *The Bible as History*, Hodder & Stoughton, London, 1974, pp 386–7

Endnotes

36 F W Farrar, *The Life of Christ*, Cassell and Company, London, 1900, p 513

37 ibid, p 514

38 Daniel 9:24–27. See also 11:30–33

39 J McDowell, *Evidence That Demands a Verdict*, Thomas Nelson, Nashville, Tennessee, 1979, pp 170–5. See also D Ford, *Daniel*, Southern Publishing Association, Nashville, Tennessee, 1978, pp 225–38

40 Matthew 24:15–16. See also Luke 21:20–21

41 C H Moore and J Jackson (translators), *Tacitus*, Harvard University Press, Cambridge, Massachusetts, 1937, (Annals, XII:38, 43, 64; XV:22; XVI:10–13)

42 Farrar, op cit, pp 478–9

43 Keller, op cit, pp 513–4

44 See for example Keller, op cit, pp 386–9 and Farrar, op cit, pp 513–4

45 H St J Thackeray and R Marcus (translators), *Josephus*, Harvard University Press, Cambridge, Massachusetts, 1943

46 J B Payne, *Encyclopaedia of Biblical Prophecy*, Baker Books, Grand Rapids, Michigan, 1997

47 J Mc Dowell, op cit

48 Ezekiel 26:3

49 Ezekiel, 26:7–9

50 Ezekiel, 26:4

51 Ezekiel, 26:12, 14

52 Ezekiel, 26:14, 21

53 Ezekiel, 28:22–23

54 J F C Fuller and E D Grohman, 'Tyre', *Encyclopaedia Britannica*, Encyclopaedia Britannica Inc, Chicago, 1967, vol 22, pp 452–3. See also J McDowell, op cit, p 275

55 Ezekiel 29:19–20

56 J F C Fuller and E D Grohman, op cit

57 J McDowell, op cit, pp 277–8

58 J F C Fulller and E D Grohman, op cit

59 J McDowell, op cit, pp 277–8

60 R D Barnett, 'Sidon', *Encyclopaedia Britannica*, Encyclopaedia Britannica Inc, Chicago, 1967, vol 20, p 483

61 J McDowell, op cit, pp 267–323. See also Payne, op cit

62 E Cheetham, *The Prophecies of Nostradamus*, Corgi Books, London, 1973, p 93

63 Ibid p 94

64 C A Ronan, 'Nostradamus', *Encyclopaedia Britannica*, Encyclopaedia Britannica Inc 1967, vol 16, p 663

65 M Gauquelin, *Dreams and Illusions of Astrology*, Prometheus Books, Buffalo, New York, 1979, pp 132–5. See also E Cheetham, op cit, p 82

66 ibid, p 126

67 Gauquelin, op cit, p 130

68 Cheetham, op cit, p 38

69 Gauquelin, op cit, p 130

70 ibid pp 130–40

71 R Montgomery, *A Gift of Prophecy, The Phenomenal Jeane Dixon*, Bantam Books, New York, 1966, p 6

72 N Blundell, The Supernatural, Promotional Reprint Co Ltd, London, 1996, p 96

73 R Montgomery, op cit, pp 76,81–2, 144–5

74 ibid, p 39. See also p 38

75 ibid, p 193. See also pp 179–81 and 192–5
76 ibid, p 101
77 P Davies, *The Mind of God*, Simon & Schuster, London, 1992, pp 154–5
78 Y M Lanhers, 'Saint Joan', *Encyclopaedia Britannica*, Encyclopaedia Britannica Inc, 1967, vol 13, pp 3–7. See also F W H Myers, *Proceedings of the Society for Psychical Research*, vol V, 1888–89, pp 543–5; and Glass, op cit, pp 72–5
79 Lanhers, op cit, p 6
80 S Freud, 'Dreams and Telepathy', in *Psychoanalysis and the Occult*, G Devereax (ed), International Universities Press, New York, 1953, p 86. See also C Jung, *Dreams*, Princeton University Press, Princeton, New Jersey, 1974, p 47; W Stekel, *The Interpretation of Dreams*, Grosset and Dunlap, New York, 1962, p 552; M Boss, *The Analysis of Dreams*, Philosophical Library, New York, 1958, p 182
81 R L Van de Castle, *Our Dreaming Mind*, Ballantine Books, New York, 1994, pp 411–2
82 J Taylor, *Science and the Supernatural*, Paladin Books, London, 1980, p 177

Chapter 3

1 R Montgomery, *A Gift of Prophecy:The Phenomenal Jeane Dixon*, Bantam, New York, 1966, pp 6, 81–3
2 F Hartmann, *Paracelsus: Life and Prophecies*, Rudolf Steiner Publications, Blauvelt, New York, 1973, p 105
3 R Sheldrake, 'Are You Looking At Me', in *New Scientist*, 26 July 1997, p 39
4 J B Rhine, JG Pratt, B Smith, C Stuart, and J Greenwood, *Extra-Sensory Perception After Sixty Years*, Bruce Humphries, Boston, 1966
5 J Taylor, *Science and the Supernatural*, Granada, London, 1980, pp 56–8
6 ibid, p 58
7 ibid
8 R Targ and H Puthoff, 'Information Transmission Under Conditions of Sensory Shielding', in *Nature*, vol 251, 18 October 1974, pp 602–7
9 Taylor, op cit, pp 60–1
10 Targ & Puthoff, op cit
11 A Hastings and D Hurt, 'A Confirmatory Remote Viewing in a Group Setting', in *Proceedings of the IEEE*, vol 64, October 1976, pp 1544–54. See also CT Tart, HE Puthoff and R Targ, *Mind at Large*, Praeger Publishers, New York, 1979
12 R G Jahn (ed), *The Role of Consciousness in the Physical World*, Westview Press Inc, Boulder, Colorado, 1981, pp 37–86
13 J McCrone, 'Roll Up for the Telepathy Test', in *New Scientist*, 15 May 1993, pp 29–33
14 R Matthews, 'Blind Prejudice', in *New Scientist*, 17 January 1998, p 12
15 Bem D J and Honorton C, 'Does Psi Exist? Replicable Evidence for an Anomalous Process of Information Transfer', in *Psychological Bulletin*, vol 115, 1994, pp 44–8
16 McCrone, op cit
17 ibid
18 C T Tart, HE Puthoff and R Targ, op cit, pp 107–24. See also B J Dunne and J Bisaha, 'Precognitive Remote Viewing in the Chicago Area: A Replication of the Stanford Experiments', in *Journal of Parapsychology* Vol 43, March 1979, pp 17–30
19 R G Jahn and B J Dunne, *Margins of Reality*, Harcourt Brace Jovanovich, San Diego, 1987, pp 151–6

20 ibid, pp 162–3
21 ibid, pp 164–5
22 ibid, pp 166–7
23 ibid, pp 172–3
24 ibid, pp 168–9
25 ibid, pp 181, 185
26 ibid, p 187
27 ibid, p 188
28 ibid
29 ibid, pp 188–9
30 Taylor, op cit, p 181
31 ibid, p 58
32 I Stevenson, 'Precognition of Disasters', in *Journal of the American Society of Psychical Research*, vol 64, 1970, pp 187–210

Chapter 4

1 F Urquhart, *The Monarch Butterfly: International Traveller*, Nelson Hall, Chicago, 1987
2 S M Perez, O R Taylor and R Jander, 'A Sun Compass in Monarch Butterflies', in *Nature*, vol 387, 1997, p 29
3 J Poirier, 'The Magnificent Migrating Monarch', in *Creation*, vol 20, No1, December 1997–February 1998, pp 28–31. See also J Poirier, *From Darkness to Light to Flight: Monarch–the Miracle Butterfly*, Institute for Creation Research, El Cajon, California, 1997
4 M Ricard, *The Mystery of Animal Migration*, Constable, London, 1969
5 K Von Frisch, *Animal Architecture*, Hutchinson, London, 1975
6 R Sheldrake, *A New Science of Life*, Paladin, London, 1987
7 ibid, pp 20–34 and 202–10
8 N Herbert, 'How to Be in Two Places at One Time', in *New Scientist*, 21 August 1986, pp 41–4. See also P C W Davies and J R Brown, *The Ghost in the Atom*, Cambridge University Press, Cambridge, 1987, pp 40–4
9 E Squires, *The Mystery of the Quantum World*, Adam Holger, Bristol, 1986, pp 32–3
10 ibid, p 37
11 Davies and Brown, op cit, p 8
12 See, for example, J C Polkinghorne, *The Quantum World*, Penguin Books, Harmondsworth, England, 1987, p 37. See also Davies and Brown, op cit, p 8–13
13 D Bohm, *Wholeness and the Implicate Order*, Ark Paperbacks, London, 1988, pp 79–84. See also N Herbert, *Quantum Reality*, Rider, London, 1985, pp 49–50, 188–9; Davies and Brown, op cit, pp 126–9
14 Davies and Brown, op cit, pp 126–9
15 P Davies, *Superforce*, Unwin Paperbacks, London, 1987, pp 220–1
16 W Hasker, *God, Time, and Knowledge*, Cornell University Press, Ithaca, 1989, pp 58–9
17 M A Lewis, 'Armada', in *Encyclopaedia Britannica*, Encyclopaedia Britannica Inc, Chicago, 1967, vol 2, pp 415–6
18 M B Jansen, 'Japan', in *Encylopedia Britannica*, op cit, vol 12, p 897
19 R Heymans, *The Voortrekker Monument, Pretoria*, Board of Control of the Voortrekker

Monument, Pretoria, 1986. See also *The Battles of Sandlwana and Rorke's Drift—Shiyane*, Natal Provincial Museum Service and KwaZulu Monuments Council, Rorke's Drift, 1993

20 H Butterfield, *Christianity and History*, Fontana Books, London, 1958, p 143

21 R S Laura, 'Towards a New Theology of Trancendence', in *Sophia (Australia)*, vol 25, 1986, pp 30–40

22 J Lovelock, *The Ages of Gaia*, Oxford University Press, Oxford, 1989

23 For a more detailed account of the experimental evidence see R G Jahn and B J Dunne, *Margins of Reality*, Harcourt Brace Jovanovich, San Diego, 1988, pp 85–148

24 L J Henderson, *The Fitness of the Environment*, Peter Smith, Gloucester, Massachusetts, 1970

25 J D Barrow and F J Tipler, *The Anthropic Cosmological Principle*, Oxford University Press, Oxford, 1988

26 J D Barrow and J Silk, *The Left Hand of Creation*, Heinemann, London, 1983, p 207

27 ibid, p 227

28 W Gitt, *In the Beginning was Information*, CLV Chrisliche Literatur–Vertreitung e V , Bielefeld, 1997

29 L M Spetner, *Not By Chance*, The Judaica Press, New York, 1997, p vii

30 J Knight, 'Top Translator', in *New Scientist*, 18 April 1998, p 15

31 P Davies, *The Cosmic Blueprint*, Unwin Paperbacks, London, 1989, p 160. See also P Davies, 'Chaos Free the Universe', in *New Scientist*, 6 October, 1990, pp 36–9

32 M J Behe, *Darwin's Black Box*, The Free Press, New York, 1996, pp 173–86

33 ibid, pp 185–86

34 ibid, p 187

35 ibid

36 A Snelling, 'Radioactive 'dating' in conflict', in *Creation*, vol 20, no 1, December 1997–February 1998, pp 24–7

37 G B Dalrymple, '40Ar 36Ar Analyses of Historical Lava Flows' in *Earth and Planetary Letters*, vol 6, 1969, pp 47–55

38 J G Funkhouser and J J Naughton, 'Radiogenic Helium and Argon in Ultramafic Inclusions from Hawaii', in *Journal of Geophysical Research*, vol 73, no 14, July 1968, pp 4601–7

39 S A Austin, *Grand Canyon: Monument to Catastrophe*, Institute for Creation Research, Santee, California, 1994, pp 111–131

40 A A Snelling, 'The Failure of U-Th-Pb 'Dating' at Koongarra, Australia', in *Creation Ex Nihlo Technical Journal*, vol 9, no 1, 1996, pp 71–92

41 ibid, pp 71, 91

42 P A L Giem *Scientific Theology*, La Sierra University Press, Riverside, California, 1997, pp 111–190

43 J D Morris, *The Young Earth*, Green Forest, Arizona, 1997, pp 73–117

44 D A Leeming and M A Leeming, *A Dictionary of Creation Myths*, Oxford University Press, New York, 1994. See also A M Rehwinkel, *The Flood in the Light of the Bible, Geology and Archaeology*, Concordia Publishing House, Saint Louis, Missouri, 1951, pp 127–64

45 H R Schoolcraft, *History of the Indian Tribes of the United States*, J B Lippincott and Co, Philadelphia, 1857, vol 6, p 571 (cited in S A Austin, op cit, p 205)

46 L Pierce, 'The Forgotten Archbishop', in *Creation*, vol 20, no 2, March–May 1998, pp 42–3

47 R H Mathews, *Chinese–English Dictionary*, Harvard University Press, Cambridge,

Massachusetts, 1975, p 1165. See also W Shih-Ch'ang, 'Chronology 1 Chinese', in *Encyclopaedia Britannica*, Encyclopaedia Britannica Inc, Chicago, 1967, vol 5, p 720

48 L C Goodrich, 'China 1 Origins', in *Encyclopaedia Britannica*, Encyclopaedia Britannica Inc, Chicago, 1967, vol 5, pp 574–5

49 J Baines and J Malek, *Atlas of Ancient Egypt*, Time-Life Books, Amsterdam, 1995, p 8

50 P James, I J Thorpe, N Kokkinos, R Morkot and J Frankish, *Centuries of Darkness: A Challenge to the Conventional Chronology of Old World Archaeology*, Jonathon Cape, London, 1992. See also I Velikovsky, *Ages in Chaos*, Sidgwick and Jackson, London, 1971 and 'Another Nail in the Chronology Coffin', *Archaeological Diggings*, June–July 1996, pp 18–23

51 C L Woolley, 'Ur', in *Encylopaedia Britannica*, Encyclopaedia Britannica Inc, Chicago, 1967, Vol 22, pp 773–5

52 A B Paine, *Mark Twain: A Biography*, Harper and Brothers, New York, 1912, pp 134 (cited by I Stevenson, 'Precognition of Disasters', in *Journal of the American Society of Psychical Research*, vol 64, 1970, pp 187–210)

53 D Bohm, *Wholeness and the Implicate Order*, Ark Paperbacks, London, 1988

54 S Bains, 'Into the Third Dimension', in *New Scientist*, 19 July 1997, pp 28–32

55 E N Leith and J Upatnicks, 'Photography by Laser', in *Scientific American*, vol 212, no 6, June 1965, pp 24–35

56 K H Pribram, *Languages of the Brain*, Prentice-Hall Inc, Englewood Cliffs, New Jersey, 1971

57 K Wilber (ed), *The Holographic Paradigm and Other Paradoxes: Exploring the Leading Edge of Science*, New Scientist Library, Shambhala, Boulder, Colorado, 1982

58 S Grof, *Ancient Wisdom and Modern Science*, State of University of New York Press, Albany, New York, 1984

59 E J Larson and L Witham, 'Scientists Are Still Keeping the Faith', in *Nature*, vol 386, 1997, pp 435–6

60 S Harris, 'Why I am a new believer', in *The Sunday Telegraph* (Sydney), 15 March 1998, p 55

Chapter 5

1 Daniel, 2:1–35

2 Daniel, 2:36–45

3 Daniel, 2:46–48

4 *The History of Herodotus*, Book 1: 152, 154, William Benton, Publisher, Chicago, 1952

5 Daniel, 8:1–8

6 Daniel, 8:15–22

7 V L Ehrenberg, 'Hellenistic Age', in *Encyclopaedia Britannica*, Encyclopaedia Britannica Inc, Chicago, 1967, vol 11, p 324

8 E Gibbon, *The History of the Decline and Fall of the Roman Empire*, Methuen and Co, London, 1900, vol 4, p 161

9 D Ford, *Daniel*, Southern Publishing Association, Nashville, Tennessee, 1978 pp 30–44

10 See, for example, *The History of Herodotus*, op cit, book 1:184. See also C J Gadd, 'Semiramis', in *Encyclopaedia Britannica*, Encyclopaedia Britannica Inc, Chicago, 1967, vol 20, pp 207–8

11 M E L Mallowan, 'Babylon', in *Encyclopaedia Britannica*, Encyclopaedia Britannica Inc, Chicago, 1967, vol 2, pp 949–51

12 Daniel, 5:1–30

13 D J Wiseman, 'Belshazzar', in *Encyclopaedia Britannica*, Encyclopaedia Britannica Inc, Chicago, 1967, vol 3, p 458

14 *Cyropaedia*, book vii, 5, 10, 13, 15, 16, 26–30

15 Daniel, 5:17–23

16 See, for example, Daniel, 7:9–10, 12:1–3

17 Ford, op cit, pp 25–27

18 Daniel, 5:29. See also reference 13

19 *The History of Herodotus*, op cit, Book 1, 191

20 F Josephus, *The Antiquities of the Jews*, Book 11, Ch 8, in W Whiston (ed) *The Complete Works of the Learned and Authentic Jewish Historian Flavius Josephus*, J F Tallis, London, undated, pp 237–8

21 ibid

22 ibid

23 ibid

24 Leviticus

25 Leviticus, 25:1–7

26 Jeremiah, 25:8–12

27 2 Chronicles 36:21

28 E F Siegman, 'Saul', in *Encyclopaedia Britannica*, Encyclopaedia Britannica Inc, Chicago, 1967, vol 19, p 1096

29 P Davies, *God and the New Physics*, Penguin Books, Harmondsworth, Middlesex, 1987, p 222

30 Daniel, 9:20–27

31 Ford, op cit, p 198. See also I Newton, *Observations Upon the Prophecies of Daniel*, James Nisbet, London, 1831

32 Ford, op cit, pp 228–32

33 Daniel, 9:26–27

34 Ford, op cit, p 238

35 ibid, pp 239–84

36 Daniel, op cit, 12:1–3

37 Daniel, 7:9–10, 22. See also 2:44–45

38 Victorinus, *Works*, R E Wallis (translator), in *The Ante-Nicene Fathers : Translations of the Writings of the Fathers Down to AD 325*, Charles Scribner's Sons, New York, 1899–1926, vol 7, p 353

39 The Revelation to John , 1:10–11

40 Ibid, 11:17–18

41 Ibid, 19:11–21

42 Ibid, 20:4–15

43 Genesis 1:1 to 2:3

44 S J Case, *The Millennial Hope*, The University of Chicago Press, Chicago, Illinois, 1918, pp 19–23. See also J Duchesne–Guillemin, 'Zoroastrrianism', in *Encyclopaedia Britannica*, Encyclopaedia Britannica Inc, Chicago, 1967, vol 23, pp 1015–8

45 S G Morley, *The Ancient Maya*, Stanford University Press, Palo Alto, California, 1956, p 236

46 M Leon-Portilla, *Time and Reality in the Thought of the Maya*, Beacon Press, Boston, 1973, pp 107–8

Endnotes

47 Morley, op cit, pp 51–5, 188, 242

48 S G Morley, G W Brainerd and R J Sharer, *The Ancient Maya*, Stanford University Press, Palo Alto, California, 1983, pp 556, 603. See also J E S Thompson, *Maya Hieroglyphic Writing*, University of Oklahoma Press, Norman, Oklahoma, 1960, Appendix 4, pp 314–6

49 H G Guinness, *Light For the Last Days: A Study Historic and Prophetic*, Hodder & Stoughton, London, 1888, pp 221–5

50 ibid, p 222

51 H Kohn, 'Zionism', in *Encyclopaedia Britannica*, Encyclopaedia Britannica Inc, Chicago, 1967, vol 23, pp 980–1

52 Leviticus, 25:8–17

53 See, for example, G Curle, *Times of the Signs*, New Wine Press, Chichester, England, 1988; and A G Gilbert and Maurice M Cotterell, *The Mayan Prophecies*, Element, Shaftesbury, Dorset, 1997

54 F D Nichol, 'Miller, William', in *Encyclopaedia Britannica*, Encyclopaedia Britannica Inc, Chicago, 1967, vol 15, p 466

55 Daniel, 8:13–14

56 H M J Loewe and C Roth, 'Jews II Earliest Times to AD 135, C Greek and Roman Conquests' in *Encyclopaedia Britannica*, Encyclopaedia Britannica Inc, Chicago, 1967, Vol 12, p 1062. See also Ford, op cit, pp 188–90, 196–7

Chapter 6

1 See, for example, W Hasker, *God, Time, and Knowledge*, Cornell University Press, Ithaca, 1989

2 See, for example, D Basinger and R Basinger, (eds), *Predestination and Free Will: Four Views of Divine Sovereignty and Human Freedom*, Inter Varsity Press, Downers Grove, Illinois, 1986; P Geach, *Providence and Evil*, Cambridge University Press, Cambridge, 1977

3 'Granicus, Battle of the', *Encyclopaedia Britannica*, Encyclopaedia Britannica Inc, Chicago, 1967, Vol 10, p 682

4 See, for example, H Price, *Angels, True Stories of How they Touch our Lives*, Macmillan, London, 1993; C W Shedd, *Brush of an Angel's Wing*, Servant Publications, Ann Arbor, Michigan, 1994; E L Martin, *I Saw God's Hand*, Amazing Facts, Inc, Frederick, Maryland 1973

5 J Boslough, *Beyond the Black Hole*, Collins, London, 1985, p 109

6 C Beckett, 'The Great Chain of Being', *New Scientist*, 24 March 1990, pp 46–7

7 For a detailed assessment of the damage to our environment caused by our technology and the wastes it produces see, for example, J F Ashton and R S Laura, *The Perils of Progress*, University of New South Wales Press, Sydney, 1998

8 E R Nelson and R E Broadberry, *Genesis and the Mystery Confucius Couldn't Solve*, Concordia Publishing House, Saint Louis, 1994

9 Confucius, *The Doctrine of The Mean*, xix, 6, (cited by ibid, p 1)

Further Reading

Ashton, J F, and Laura, R S, *The Perils of Progress*, University of New South Wales Press, Sydney, 1998

Baines, J and Malek, J, *Atlas of Ancient Egypt*, Time-Life Books, Amsterdam, 1995

Bains, S, 'Into the Third Dimension', in *New Scientist*, 19 July 1997, pp 28–32

Barrow, J D, and Silk, J, *The Left Hand of Creation*, Heinemann, London, 1983

Barrow, J D, and Tipler, F J, *The Anthropic Cosmological Principle*, Oxford University Press, Oxford, 1988

Basinger, D, and Basinger, R, (eds), *Predestination and Free Will: Four Views of Divine Sovereignty and Human Freedom*, Inter Varsity Press, Downers Grove, Illinois, 1986

Beckett, C, 'The Great Chain of Being', in *New Scientist*, 24 March 1990

Behe, M J, *Darwin's Black Box*, The Free Press, New York, 1996

Bem, D J and Honorton, C, 'Does Psi Exist? Replicable Evidence for an Anomalous Process of Information Transfer', in *Psychological Bulletin*, vol 115, 1994

Bietak, M, 'Egypt and Canaan During the Middle Bronze Age', in *Bulletin of the American Schools of Oriental Research*, vol 281, 1991

Bietak, M, *Avaris: The Capital of the Hyksos*, British Museum Press, London, 1996

Blomefield, E, 'The Swaffham Tinker', in R L Woods (ed), *The World of Dreams*, Random House, New York, 1947

Blundell, N, *The Supernatural*, Promotional Reprint Co Ltd, London, 1996

Bohm, D, *Wholeness and the Implicate Order*, Ark Paperbacks, London, 1988

Boslough, J, *Beyond the Black Hole*, Collins, London, 1985

Boss, M, *The Analysis of Dreams*, Philosophical Library, New York, 1958

Bradford, S, *Harriet Tubman: The Moses of Her People*, Peter Smith, Gloucester, Massachusetts, 1981

Butterfield, H, *Christianity and History*, Fontana Books, London, 1958

Carson, B and Murphey, C, *Gifted Hands*, Review and Herald Publishing Association, Washington DC 1990

Case, S J, *The Millennial Hope*, University of Chicago Press, Chicago, Illinois, 1918

Cheetham, E, *The Prophecies of Nostradamus*, Corgi Books, London, 1973

Cohen, J, 'That's Amazing, Isn't It?', in *New Scientist*, 17 January, 1998

Cohen, J, and Stewart, I, *Figments of Reality*, Cambridge University Press, Cambridge, 1977

Cremin, A (ed), *The Enduring Past*, New South Wales University Press, New South Wales, 1988

Curle, G, *Times of the Signs*, New Wine Press, Chichester, England, 1988

Dalrymple, G B, '40Ar 36Ar Analyses of Historical Lava Flows' in *Earth and Planetary Letters*, vol 6, 1969

Davies, P C W, and Brown, J R, *The Ghost in the Atom*, Cambridge University Press, Cambridge, 1987

Davies, P, 'Chaos Free the Universe', in *New Scientist*, 6 October, 1990

Davies, P, *God and the New Physics*, Penguin Books, Harmondsworth, Middlesex, 1987

Further Reading

Davies, P, *Superforce*, Unwin Paperbacks, London, 1987

Davies, P, *The Cosmic Blueprint*, Unwin Paperbacks, London, 1989

Davies, P, *The Mind of God*, Simon & Schuster, London, 1992

de Becker, R, *The Understanding of Dreams and Their Influence on the History of Man*, Hawthorn Books, New York, 1968

Down, D K, 'The Pyramids of Egypt', in *Archaeological Diggings*, April/May, 1997

Dunne, B J and Bisaha, J, 'Precognitive Remote Viewing in the Chicago Area: A Replication of the Stanford Experiments', in *Journal of Parapsychology* Vol 43, March 1979

Edwards, I E S, *The Pyramids of Egypt*, Penguin Books (originally published 1947)

English, J, 'A Scientist's Experience with Tarot', in J Wanless and A Arrien (eds), *The Wheel of Tarot: A New Revolution*, Merrill-West Publishers, Carmel, California, 1993

Fagen, M (ed), *A History of Engineering and Science in the Bell System: National Service in War and Peace (1925–1975)*, Bell Telephone Laboratories, Murry Hill, New York, 1978

Farrar, F W, *The Life of Christ*, Cassell and Company, London, 1900

Ford, D, Daniel, Southern Publishing Association, Nashville, Tennessee, 1978

Freud, S 'Dreams and Telepathy', in G Devereax (ed), *Psychoanalysis and the Occult*, International Universities Press, New York, 1953

Funkhouser, J G, and Naughton, J J, 'Radiogenic Helium and Argon in Ultramafic Inclusions from Hawaii', in *Journal of Geophysical Research*, vol 73, no 14, July 1968

Gandhi, M, *An Autobiography: The Story of My Experiments With Truth*, Beacon Press, Boston, 1957

Gauquelin, M, *Dreams and Illusions of Astrology*, Prometheus Books, Buffalo, New York, 1979

Geach, P, *Providence and Evil*, Cambridge University Press, Cambridge, 1977

Gibbon, E, *The History of the Decline and Fall of the Roman Empire*, Methuen and Co, London, 1900, vol 4

Gilbert, A G, and Cotterell, Maurice M, *The Mayan Prophecies*, Element, Shaftesbury, Dorset, 1997

Gitt, W, *In the Beginning was Information*, CLV Chrisliche Literatur–Vertreitung e V, Bielefeld, 1997

Glass, J, *The Story of Fulfilled Prophecy*, Cassell, London, 1969

Grof, S, *Ancient Wisdom and Modern Science*, State of University of New York Press, Albany, New York, 1984

Guinness, H G, *Light For the Last Days: A Study Historic and Prophetic*, Hodder & Stoughton, London, 1888

Hancock, G, *Fingerprints of the Gods*, Crown Trade Paperbacks, New York, 1995

Hartmann, F, *Paracelsus: Life and Prophecies*, Rudolf Steiner Publications, Blauvelt, New York, 1973

Hasker, W, *God, Time, and Knowledge*, Cornell University Press, Ithaca, 1989

Hastings, A, and Hurt, D, 'A Confirmatory Remote Viewing in a Group Setting', in *Proceedings of the IEEE*, vol 64, October 1976

Hawkins, G S, 'Sun, Men and Stones', in *American Scientist*, vol 53, No 4, December 1965

Henderson, L J, *The Fitness of the Environment*, Peter Smith, Gloucester, Massachusetts, 1970

Herbert, N, 'How to Be in Two Places at One Time', in *New Scientist*, 21 August 1986

Herbert, N, *Quantum Reality*, Rider, London, 1985,

Heymans, R, *The Voortrekker Monument, Pretoria*, Board of Control of the Voortrekker Monument, Pretoria, 1986

Hill, B, *Gates of Horn and Ivory: An Anthology of Dreams*, Taplinger, New York, 1967

Jahn, R G and Dunne, B J, *Margins of Reality*, Harcourt Brace Jovanovich, San Diego, 1987

Jahn, R G (ed), *The Role of Consciousness in the Physical World*, Westview Press Inc, Boulder, Colorodo, 1981

James, P, Thorpe, I J, Kokkinos, Morkot, R, and Frankish, J, *Centuries of Darkness: A Challenge to the Conventional Chronology of Old World Archaeology*, Jonathon Cape, London, 1992

Jung, C, *Dreams*, Princeton University Press, Princeton, New Jersey, 1974,

Keller, W, *The Bible as History*, Hodder & Stoughton, London, 1974

Kelsey, M, *Dreams: The Dark Speech of the Spirit*, Doubleday, New York, 1968

Knight, J, 'Top Translator', in *New Scientist*, 18 April 1998

Lamon, W, 'Abraham Lincoln's Dream Life', in R L Woods (ed) *The World of Dreams*, Random House, New York, 1947

Larson, E J, and Witham, L, 'Scientists Are Still Keeping the Faith', in *Nature*, vol 386, 1997

Laura, R S, 'Towards a New Theology of Trancendence', in *Sophia (Australia)*, vol 25, 1986,

Leeming, D A, and Leeming, M A, *A Dictionary of Creation Myths*, Oxford University Press, New York, 1994

Leith, E N, and Upatnicks, J, 'Photography by Laser', in *Scientific American*, vol 212, no 6, June 1965

Leon-Portilla, M, *Time and Reality in the Thought of the Maya*, Beacon Press, Boston, 1973

Lovelock, J, *The Ages of Gaia*, Oxford University Press, Oxford, 1989

Martin, E L, *I Saw God's Hand*, Amazing Facts Inc, Frederick, Maryland 1973

Mathews, R H, *Chinese–English Dictionary*, Harvard University Press, Cambridge, Massachusetts, 1975

Matthews, R, 'Blind Prejudice', in *New Scientist*, 17 January 1998

Maxwell, A S, *Your Bible and You*, The Signs Publishing Company, Warburton, Australia, 1959

McCrone, J, 'Roll Up for the Telepathy Test', in *New Scientist*, 15 May 1993

McCusker, B, and Sutherland, C, 'Probability and the Psyche', *Journal of the Society for Psychical Research*, (London), Vol 57, January 1991

McCusker, C S, and McCusker, B, 'An Experimental Test of the Bias of Probability Theory', *Australian Physicist*, Vol 25, No 1, 1988

McDowell, J, *Evidence That Demands a Verdict*, Thomas Nelson, Nashville, Tennessee, 1979,

Miller, B, *George Muller: Man of Faith and Miracles*, Dimension Books, Minneapolis, Minnesota, 1941

Montgomery, R, *A Gift of Prophecy, The Phenomenal Jeane Dixon*, Bantam Books, New York, 1966

Moore, C H, and Jackson, J (translators), *Tacitus*, Harvard University Press, Cambridge, Massachusetts, 1937, (Annals, XII:38, 43, 64; XV:22; XVI:10–13)

Morley, S G, Brainerd, G W, and Sharer, R J, *The Ancient Maya*, Stanford University Press, Stanford, California, 1983

Morley, S, *The Ancient Maya*, Stanford University Press, Palo Alto, California, 1956

Morris, J D, *The Young Earth*, Green Forest, Arizona, 1997

Myers, F W H, *Proceedings of the Society for Psychical Research*, vol V, 1888–89

Myers, P V N, *General History for Colleges and High Schools*, Ginn and Company, Boston, 1889

Further Reading

Nelson, E R, and Broadberry, R E, *Genesis and the Mystery Confucius Couldn't Solve*, Concordia Publishing House, Saint Louis, 1994

Newbold, W, 'Sub-Conscious Reasoning', in *Proceedings of the Society for Psychical Research*, vol 12, 1886

Newton, I, *Observations Upon the Prophecies of Daniel*, James Nisbet, London, 1831

Oates, J, *Babylon*, Thames and Hudson, London, 1996

Paine, A B, *Mark Twain: A Biography*, Harper and Brothers, New York, 1912

Payne, J B, *Encyclopaedia of Biblical Prophecy*, Baker Books, Grand Rapids, Michigan, 1997

Perez, S M, Taylor, O R, and Jander, R, 'A Sun Compass in Monarch Butterflies', in *Nature*, vol 387, 1997, p 29

Pierce, L, 'The Forgotten Archbishop', in *Creation*, vol 20, no 2, March–May 1998

Poirier, J, 'The Magnificent Migrating Monarch', in *Creation*, vol 20, No 1, December 1997–February 1998

Poirier, J, *From Darkness to Light to Flight: Monarch—the Miracle Butterfly*, Institute for Creation Research, El Cajon, California, 1997

Polkinghorne, J C, *The Quantum World*, Penguin Books, Harmondsworth, England, 1987

Pribram, K H, *Languages of the Brain*, Prentice-Hall Inc, Englewood Cliffs, New Jersey, 1971

Price, H, *Angels, True Stories of How They Touch Our Lives*, Macmillan, London, 1993

Randall, J H, *The Making of the Modern Mind*, Houghton Mifflin Co , Boston, 1940

Rehwinkel, A M, *The Flood in the Light of the Bible, Geology and Archaeology*, Concordia Publishing House, Saint Louis, Missouri, 1951

Rescher, N, *Predicting the Future*, State University of New York Press, 1997

Rhine, J B, Pratt, J G, Smith, B, Stuart, C, and Greenwood, J, *Extra-Sensory Perception After Sixty Years*, Bruce Humphries, Boston, 1966

Rhine, L, *Hidden Channels of the Mind*, Sloane, New York, 1961

Ricard, M, *The Mystery of Animal Migration*, Constable, London, 1969

Roberston, M, *The Wreck of the Titan*, Pocket Books, London, 1998 (First published as *Futility* in 1898)

Rolfe, J C, *Suetonius*, William Heineman , London, 1964

Schaeffer, F A, *Death in the City*, Intervarsity Press, Chicago, 1970

Schaeffer, F A, *Pollution and the Death of Man*, Tyndale House Publishers, Wheaton, Illinois, 1981

Schindler, G, 'Dreaming of Victory', in *New Scientist*, 31 May 1997

Schoolcraft, H R, *History of the Indian Tribes of the United States*, J B Lippincott and Co, Philadelphia, 1857

Shakespeare, W, *Julius Caesar* in *The Complete Works* (Compact Edition), Clarendon Press, Oxford, 1988

Shedd, C W, *Brush of an Angel's Wing*, Servant Publications, Ann Arbor, Michigan, 1994

Sheldrake, R, 'Are You Looking At Me', in *New Scientist*, 26 July 1997

Sheldrake, R, *A New Science of Life*, Paladin, London, 1987

Sherrer, Q, *Miracles Happen When You Pray*, Zondervan Publishing House, Grand Rapids, Michigan, 1998

Snelling, A A, 'The Failure of U-Th-Pb "Dating" at Koongarra, Australia', in *Creation Ex Nihlo Technical Journal*, vol 9, no 1, 1996

Snelling, A, 'Radioactive "dating" in conflict', in *Creation*, vol 20, no 1, December 1997–February 1998

Spetner, L M, *Not By Chance*, The Judaica Press, New York, 1997

Squires, E, *The Mystery of the Quantum World*, Adam Holger, Bristol, 1986

Stekel, W, *The Interpretation of Dreams*, Grosset and Dunlap, New York, 1962

Stevenson, I, 'Precognition of Disasters', in *Journal of the American Society of Psychical Research*, vol 64, 1970

Stevenson, I, 'Seven More Paranormal Experiences Associated with the Sinking of the Titanic', in *Journal of the American Society of Psychical Research*, vol 59, 1965

Stewart, I, *Does God Play Dice*, Penguin Books, London, 1990

Talamonte, L, *Forbidden Universe*, Stein and Day, New York, 1975

Targ, R, and Puthoff, H, 'Information Transmission Under Conditions of Sensory Shielding', in *Nature*, vol 251, 18 October 1974

Tart, C T, Puthoff, H E, and Targ, R, *Mind at Large*, Praeger Publishers, New York, 1979

Taylor, J, *Science and the Supernatural*, Granada, London, 1980

Thackeray, H St J, and Marcus, R (translators), *Josephus*, Harvard University Press, Cambridge, Massachusetts, 1943

The Battles of Sandlwana and Rorke's Drift–Shiyane, Natal Provincial Museum Service and KwaZulu Monuments Council, Rorke's Drift, 1993

The History of Herodotus, Book 1, 210, William Benton, Publisher, Chicago, 1952

Thomas, K, *Religion and the Decline of Magic*, Penguin Books, London, 1984

Thompson, J E S, *Maya Hieroglyphic Writing*, University of Oklahoma Press, Norman, Oklahoma, 1960

Tibbals, G, *The Titanic: The Extraordinary Story of the Unsinkable Ship*, Reader's Digest Australia, Surry Hills, New South Wales, 1997

Urqhart, F, *The Monarch Butterfly: International Traveller*, Nelson Hall, Chicago, 1987

Van de Castle, R L, *Our Dreaming Mind*, Ballantine Books, New York, 1994

Velikovsky, I, *Ages in Chaos*, Sidgwick and Jackson, London, 1971

Von Frisch, K, *Animal Architecture*, Hutchinson, London, 1975

Wallis, R E, (translator), *The Ante-Nicene Fathers : Translations of the Writings of the Fathers Down to A D 325*, Charles Scribner's Sons, New York, 1899–1926,

Wellman, S, *Corrie Ten Boom: Heroine of Haarlem*, Barbour and Company, Uhrichsville, Ohio, 1995

Whiston, W (ed), *The Complete Works of the Learned and Authentic Jewish Historian Flavius Josephus*, J F Tallis, London, undated

White, T, 'The College', in B Hill (ed) *Such Stuff as Dreams*, Rupert Hart-Davis, London, 1967

Wilber, K (ed), *The Holographic Paradigm and Other Paradoxes: Exploring the Leading Edge of Science*, New Scientist Library, Shambhala, Boulder, Colorado, 1982

Index

Index

Index